To Sheila

for

With love. Johnny

and 1985

D1149729

THE WRITER IN DISGUISE

THE WRITER IN DISGUISE

ALAN BENNETT

faber and faber

LONDON · BOSTON

First published in 1985
by Faber and Faber Limited
3 Queen Square London WC1N 3AU

Phototypeset by Wilmaset Birkenhead
Printed in Great Britain by
Whitstable Litho Ltd., Whitstable, Kent

"I'm in love with a wonderful guy"
by Richard Rodgers and Oscar Hammerstein II
copyright 1949 Richard Rodgers & Oscar Hammerstein II
Original Publisher: Williamson Music Inc
UK Publisher: Williamson Music Ltd
Reproduced by kind permission.
"Pedro the Fisherman"
by Harry Parr Davies and Harold Purcell
copyright 1943 Chappell Music Ltd
UK Publisher: Chappell Music Ltd
Reproduced by kind permission.
"Because"
by Guy d'Hardelot and E. Teschemacher
copyright 1902 Chappell Music Ltd
UK Publisher: Chappell Music Ltd
Reproduced by kind permission.

British Library Cataloguing in Publication Data

Bennett, Alan, 1934–
The writer in disguise.
I. Title
822'.914   PR6052.E5

ISBN 0–571–13567–6

CONTENTS

The Writer in Disguise *by Alan Bennett*   9
Me, I'm Afraid of Virginia Woolf   29
All Day on the Sands   73
One Fine Day   111
The Old Crowd   159
    An Introduction *by Lindsay Anderson*   161
Afternoon Off   219

THE WRITER IN DISGUISE

Alan Bennett

These five television plays were part of a series of six produced for London Weekend Television in 1978–9.* Reading them now, five years after they were produced and six years after they were written, I can see that three of them (*Me, I'm Afraid of Virginia Woolf*, *Afternoon Off* and *One Fine Day*) are not dissimilar and that Hopkins, the polytechnic lecturer, Lee, the Chinese waiter, and Phillips, the estate agent, share the same character, indeed *are* the same character. Passive, dejected, at odds with themselves, they are that old friend, the Writer in Disguise. A doleful presence, whatever his get-up, he slips apologetically in and out of scenes being heartfelt, while the rest of the cast, who are invariably more fun (and more fun to write, too), get on with the business of living. They are not heartfelt at all; one doesn't have to be fair to them, nor are they around long enough to elicit understanding. And, unlike the sorry hero, they *talk*. But it's hard to find words to put into the mouth of the central character when "Gr–rr–rr" or "Oh dear" seem to say it all. Lee, the Chinese waiter, who scarcely speaks but only smiles is the ineffectual hero taken to a logical conclusion and the natural condition of all three is what Lee ends up doing – namely, lying in his underpants staring at the ceiling.

What distinguishes a television play from a stage play I find hard to say. It's plain that of these plays only *The Old Crowd* could conceivably have been presented on the stage because it's the only

* The sixth, *Doris and Doreen* is included in *Office Suite*, published by Faber and Faber Ltd, 1981.

one not set in a variety of locations, besides being written in a deliberately theatrical way. The empty house in *The Old Crowd* is a kind of stage, and whereas the other plays are in varying degrees naturalistic *The Old Crowd* is not naturalistic at all (which may explain why it annoyed so many viewers and was generally disliked). The difference between writing for stage and for television is almost an optical one. Language on the stage has to be slightly larger than life because it is being heard in a much larger space. Plot counts for less on the television screen because one is seeing the characters at closer quarters than in the theatre. The shape and plot of a stage play count for more in consequence of the distance between the audience and the action. A theatre audience has a perspective on a play as a television audience does not. The audience in a theatre is an entity as a television audience is not. On television the playwright is conversing. In the theatre he is (even when conversing) addressing a meeting. The stage aspires to the condition of art as television seldom does (which is not to say that it shouldn't). The most that can be said for these plays in that respect is that occasionally they stray into literature.

Of the five scripts printed here three were shot wholly on film (*Afternoon Off*, *One Fine Day* and *All Day on the Sands*); one in the studio wholly on tape (*The Old Crowd*) with the other (*Me, I'm Afraid of Virginia Woolf*) a mixture of both. If I prefer working on film to working in the studio it is for entirely frivolous reasons. Being on location with a unit, like being on tour with a play, concentrates the experience; one is beleaguered, often enjoyably so, and for a short while the film becomes the framework of one's life. I am more gregarious than I like to think and to be working on a film with congenial people in an unfamiliar place seems to me the best sort of holiday. In the studio this camaraderie and shared concern is more circumscribed. There are homes to go to, lives to be lived and the recording process is altogether more routine. For the studio staff it may be a play for today, but tomorrow it's *The South Bank Show* and the day after *Game for a Laugh*. It's work in a way that filming on location, however arduous, never quite is.

Not that it is often arduous. To an onlooker, which for much of the time I am, it's like war: long periods of boredom punctuated by bouts of frenzied activity. The scene in Tony Richardson's *The Charge of the Light Brigade* in which Lord Raglan and his party view the charge from a nearby hilltop is (perhaps deliberately) very like watching the making of a film. The terminology of film (cut, shoot, action, reload) is the terminology of battle and it is a battle in which the director is the general and the actors are infantry, never told what is happening, left hanging about for hours at a time, then suddenly, because "the light is right", on standby, ready to go. Troops in the trenches used to stand to when the light was right; actors share their pessimism and the sense that, though seldom consulted, they are the ones who must get up and do it. The director is staff; he is behind the gun. The actors face it. And it isn't simply a metaphor. There is a lot of playing soldiers about it. Forget film – there would be many directors just as happy conducting a small war.

How well these scripts *read* I'm not sure. Strictly speaking there is no such thing as a good script, only a good film, a good play. But though a script is only a partial document, a guide to what ends up on the screen, I'm old-fashioned enough to have more faith in the permanence of print than of any other medium: tapes can be wiped, films lost. Television has been going full blast now for more than thirty years without the BBC or ITV working out a foolproof archive system. Besides, these plays went out once only and on a Saturday night opposite *Match of the Day*, which is virtually a recipe for oblivion, so I'm happy to see them rescued and printed here.

I owe a good deal to Stephen Frears, who produced all five plays and directed three of them, to Lindsay Anderson and Giles Foster who directed the others, and also to George Fenton who scored them all. Writing incidental music for films is a thankless task precisely because most of the time it has to be incidental. But occasionally it's crucial and then the writer or the director as like as not get the credit for the effect of scenes the composer has brought off or (more likely) has had to rescue: the entry of each character in *The Old Crowd* on the page seems quite flat and would have done so in the film without the lilting tune, both sad and silly that comes in with them. Lindsay Anderson has written his own account of directing *The Old Crowd* and the extracts from my diary that follow give some flavour of what working on that and the other plays was like.

WEDNESDAY, II JANUARY 1978

London: *The Old Crowd*

Lindsay Anderson lives in a flat in one of the redbrick turn-of-the-century blocks behind John Barnes in Swiss Cottage. With its solid turreted houses, backing on gardens, Canfield, Compayne, Aberdare, Broadhurst, it's the haunt of refugees and Jewish old ladies, and perhaps (Lindsay would strike out that "perhaps") the most European bit of London.

Lindsay comes to the door in a plastic apron in the middle of preparing leeks or parsnips. He makes me some coffee, then we sit at the kitchen table and work on the script. He looks at me enquiringly, then puts a straight line through half a page. "Boring, don't you think? Too tentative." He invariably crosses out all my "possiblys" and "perhapses". To be epic is, if nothing else, to be positive. He agreed to do the *The Old Crowd* in the first place because he detected "epic" qualities in it. I think this is to do with the house being completely bare and with George and Betty, the middle-class couple, not letting anything interfere with their intention to have a party. Lindsay wants the script to be more epic, but I am still not sure what epic means. "The doors all open downstairs when everybody has gone. That is epic." I think it means things do not have to be explained, but am not sure of the difference between this and mystification. I don't say this. Sometimes I resent seeing a day's work crossed out at a stroke (except that I can generally salvage it for something else). It is like having one's homework marked, and there is a lot of the schoolmaster about him, and some of wanting to please the teacher about me. Every few minutes work stops and gossip takes over. "You didn't like that?" (Incredulously, mouth set in a long firm line.) The eyes close in despair and he shakes his head. "And I can't stand *him*. So *English*." "English" is invariably a word of abuse, representing smallness of mind, intimacy, gossip, charm. All the things Auden fled from. Yet Lindsay is himself very English. Sometimes he routs out his scrapbook to illustrate a point. There is a picture of the Archbishop of Canterbury gingerly touching the bone threaded through the nose of some Zulu warrior. Peter Hall's Sanderson advert. Many telephone calls. Alan Bates. William Douglas-Home. Michael Medwin. Actors wanting advice about their lives (which he gives) accompanied by an elaborate pantomime of despair for my benefit.

The flat is airy and comfortable. A corridor lined with photographs, but not, as in my house, picked up at junk shops. His own school. His own life. Lindsay as a child in India astride an enormous gun. Pre-war gym displays at Cheltenham College. Awards for films and for commercials. A pinboard on which is a picture of Brecht, a photo of the cast of *What the Butler Saw*. Lindsay directing Ralph Richardson. A group photo of some critics. "Look at them, Alan. I mean, is it surprising?" He shakes his head. "England." In the lavatory a jokey warning notice. (He is not afraid of conforming to type even when the type is a bit of a joke.) He has no pretensions to taste and would presumably despise the word. Dozens of bottles of slivovitz and vodka in the kitchen, souvenirs of visits to Eastern Europe. Odd bits of peasant art. A poster of a Polish film festival. Solid, plumpish, with his long nose and wide mouth, Lindsay looks quite Polish himself. Coffee over he starts preparing my lunch. He is a hospitable man, though the odd thing is he prepares my lunch separately from his and serves it first, though his consists of the same ingredients.

We have finished the script now. He has suggested only small sections of dialogue, but dealt more positively with the characters than I would dare to: had Totty die in the drawing room; sent the waiters mysteriously into the night. At the moment we are hung up on the music. I wanted the entertainers who come to the house to sing, very formally, the song from *High Noon* ("Do not forsake me, O my darling"). Lindsay wants something much straighter, more "cultural".

At another point he wants all the guests to sing a song round the dead body of Totty, the uninvited guest who collapses and dies in the middle of a slide show. He suggests "The Sun Shines Bright" from the John Ford film, a song that has happy associations for him. It has none for me. Or not quite none. It brings back a terrible film about Stephen Foster that I saw as a child at the Crown down Tong Road in Leeds. We joke about these songs and no decision is reached, except that Lindsay goes round softly crooning "The Sun Shines Bright" in the hope I will get to like it.

He doesn't understand jokes. Or why people make them. "No, I don't like jokes," he admits. "Wisecracks, yes. Jokes, no. Have you heard there's a new punk rock group. They perform in Brady and Hindley masks and call themselves 'The Moors Murderers'. That's why we can't have satire in England."

"Never mind," he says as I go. "This will just be thought of as a small hiccup in your career."

I'm enjoying it.

SATURDAY, 11 FEBRUARY 1978

London: *The Old Crowd*

A runthrough of *The Old Crowd* in the Territorial Army Drill Hall in Handel Street, Bloomsbury. Whereas I had thought it bitty and formless and without point or humour I see now much of it works, particularly when the actors have the courage to declaim the lines and not invest them with too much heart or meaning. John Moffatt is particularly good and Jill Bennett very stylish. The play's greatest virtue is that it does not seem like mine.

Rachel Roberts and Jill Bennett go off to lunch together to compare notes on their various husbands. They are like old-fashioned stars, both in expensive fur coats, and when together sly and mischievous and in league against men.

Lindsay has no false pride. He will consider suggestions from anybody. "Grateful for them. I mean, come on. One has few enough ideas of one's own." He is often accused of cribbing from Buñuel, but has actually seen very few Buñuel films. People have told him about them, though. "That gives you a much more vivid picture. I don't think I want to see them in case I'm disappointed." He believes in the creative power of mischief. At one point I suggest that Jill Bennett should say a line in a different way. "Oh yes. Tell her that. I've just told her to do the opposite. Now she won't know what to do." He turns the rehearsals into school. He is the schoolmaster alternately praising, sarcastic or self-revealing. The actors vie with each other to please him. He makes them children again so they do not mind being childish and showing their uncertainty. Stood in his cap and old windcheater he listens to them with a long-suffering air, wide mouth set in a slightly mocking smile. "Aren't they stupid? Don't you just want to shoot them all? I do. I just want to machine-gun them all." He suddenly shouts at them. "Fucking actors."

"Oh, don't start that," Jill Bennett shouts back.

"Fucking actors!"

WEDNESDAY, 22 FEBRUARY 1978

London: *The Old Crowd*

Lindsay says he doesn't like jokes but it's not true. He's not keen on wordplay or the nuances of class as reflected in dialogue but some of the nicest jokes in the script are his.

As Frank Grimes, the disreputable young butler, relieves Jill Bennett of her fur coat, his hand rests momentarily on her breast. She doesn't turn a hair but just murmurs, "Oh, thank you very much."

The party stand round the body of Totty. "I've never seen anybody dead before," says Sue brightly. "Have you?"

"Only at school," says Peter. A remark that is funny, shocking but truthful. School is exactly where he might have seen someone dead. And again it's Lindsay's line and Lindsay's life.

The only disagreement we have had has been about publicity. Lindsay believes in talking to the press at length about what he does, preparing the public for it. I've always thought that a recipe for disaster. He wins and there's a good deal in the papers. Though no one has had a chance to read the play and though it hasn't even been shot yet, he is already quite combative about it.

TUESDAY, 28 FEBRUARY 1978

Hartlepool: *Afternoon Off*

Stephen Frears shows me Seaton Carew, the seedy holiday resort near Hartlepool he thinks he may use for *Afternoon Off*. A green art deco marina, a stretch of prom, then cranes, cooling towers and a skyline filled with factories and derricks. On the shore thin Lowry figures fill sacks with sea-coal and wheel them dripping across the prom to the gates of the power station where they sell for a few shillings. Hartlepool itself has been largely flattened and a new centre built. A few of the larger buildings survive, including Baltic Chambers, a huge redbrick building with a steep pitched roof looking in the middle of the acres of rubble like the town hall at Ypres after the First World War. We wander past miles of palings and upended sleepers lining recreation grounds and allotments. The word "television" opening all doors, we are taken round the Athenaeum, a men's club. The ceiling of the pool room, where tiny old men play snooker, is cone-shaped, like the inside of a hive. The walls are lined with cues in locked tin boxes, a name painted on each. Stephen is excited, thinks I should write a new scene for the room. The young man who shows us round apologizes for it. "Although", he says happily, "it's all going to be altered soon."

MONDAY, 6 MARCH 1978

London: *All Day on the Sands*

What nobody ever says about writing is that one can spend a whole morning, like this one, just trying to think of a name . . . the name of a character, the name of a place, or, as in this case, the name of a boarding house. The boarding house has been jazzed up, made into a "private hotel", rooms give the names of Mediterranean resorts: the Portofino Room, the Marbella Lounge. What should the establishment as a whole be called?

Somerset Maugham set himself to write 2,000 words a day.

Did you ever have this problem, Somerset?

I eventually settle on the Miramar.

TUESDAY, 14 MARCH 1978

Leeds: *Me, I'm Afraid of Virginia Woolf*

A night shoot near Malvern Ground, a vast demolition site at Beeston overlooking the lights of Leeds. This is the frontier of devastation where demolition laps at the neat front doors and scoured doorsteps of solid redbrick back-to-backs. Neville Smith as Hopkins, the polytechnic lecturer, stands at a bus stop by a street lamp, the arc-lights trained on him, to say his one line at this location. It is "O my pale life!"

In Barton Grove people come to their doors, oldish mostly, couples who have lived here all their lives, lives now narrowed and attenuated by this approaching tide of destruction. I suspect that Hopkins's "O my pale life" is me presenting an edited version of my own. Located in this desperate place, observed by these bewildered people, the line insults them. I insult them.

The shot is soon done and we pack up. I imagine a similar scene, technicians coming to the bottom of a street, setting up lights as other groups arrive and stand about. A girl with a clipboard, a man with a loud hailer, waiting. Then the chief actor arrives and he is positioned under the lights, stood against a lamp standard. And shot. And not on film either. Or also on film. The technicians pack up, the cars drive away, leaving the body slumped under the lamp as the doors begin to edge open down the street.

WEDNESDAY, 15 MARCH 1978

Leeds: *Me, I'm Afraid of Virginia Woolf*

Thora Hird arrives to film the main scene of the play, in which she meets her son, Trevor, and questions him about his private life (or lack of it). We are due to film in the Civic Restaurant below the Town Hall, but shooting cannot start until it closes, so we sit in the Wharfedale Room at the Queen's Hotel having a long lunch. Thora keeps up an endless flow of reminiscence: her early days in rep, her screen test at Ealing, her time with the Crazy Gang. She was brought up in Morecambe, the daughter of the manager of the Winter Gardens. She tells of Morecambe's solitary prostitute, Nelly Hodge. How someone, going down the yard for a bucket of coal, had heard Nelly and a client going at it in the back alley. " 'Nay, Nelly,' the chap said, 'put a bit of heart into it.' And, do you know, she was eating a fish and twopennyworth at the same time." While we chat Don Revie comes in and hangs about the entrance to the kitchen. A waiter appears and gives him a parcel. He uses the Queen's Hotel as a takeaway.

The Civic Restaurant is in the basement of the Town Hall, which also houses the Crown Court. All through the long evening's filming the corridors upstairs are thronged with lawyers and policemen, awaiting the verdict in a murder trial. A twenty-year-old man is accused of battering a baby to death; there are also cigarette burns on its body. To the police and the lawyers it seems an open and shut case, but the jury has surprised everyone (and ruined all social arrangements) by staying out for seven hours. The police attribute this to the fact that the foreman of the jury is a member of the Howard League for Penal Reform and herself an unmarried mother. The judge had been hoping to go out to dinner and his Bentley waits in Victoria Street. The court caterers have gone home and eventually the judge's chamberlain lines up at Kennedy's, the film's caterers, and gets some dinner there for the judge and the high sheriff. Meanwhile the lawyers and bored policemen drift down into the basement to watch the filming and we chat.

One of the good things about being in a group, engaged in what to other people seems a glamorous activity is that I can chat to these lawyers about their job and to the policemen about theirs, behave in fact in the way writers are generally supposed to behave, but which I seldom do. I'd normally sidestep policemen and would want to keep out of the way of their prejudices lest they expect one to corroborate them, but established as part of another scene, with a setting and frame of my own, I find I am set free, enfranchised in the way people of a more outgoing temperament are all the time.

Suddenly there is a flurry of activity: the jury is being called back and the lawyers and policemen scurry back upstairs into the court. The judge's chamberlain takes me and some of the crew and puts us in the well of the court. It is like a theatrical matinee, the cast of one show going to see another. Indeed, when he follows the judge on to the bench the chamberlain gives us a little showbiz wave. The jury now file in, surprisingly informal and at ease, the men in shirtsleeves, one woman with her knitting. The judge is kind and courteous, emphasizing they must feel under no pressure to bring in a verdict. What he wants to know is whether there is any likelihood of them coming to an agreement. The foreman must answer yes or no. She asks when. "Ah," says the judge, "I mustn't answer that. That would be to put pressure on you. Obviously there will come a time when you are too tired to go on, but the very fact that you have asked that question seems to indicate to me that point has not yet been reached." It is like Oxford philosophy. The jury files out to deliberate further and out we file to do reverses on shots already filmed. I am in the corridor two hours later when the verdict comes through. A man walks through the policemen shaking his head in disgust, saying, "Manslaughter. Seven years." The prisoner was a good-looking boy. Naïvely I expected to see some depravity in his face.

We finish at 11.30 with the customary call, "Right, that's a wrap." The judge could have said the same. "Manslaughter. Seven years. And that's a wrap."

THURSDAY, 16 MARCH 1978

Leeds: *Me, I'm Afraid of Virginia Woolf*

More filming in the Town Hall, this time in a corridor which leads from the cells. Two men are led by in handcuffs, the father and uncle of a family, both deaf and dumb. The father had been sleeping with his children and allowed the uncle to do the same. Mother, father, uncle, all were deaf and dumb, but the children could speak and speech was the father's downfall. "Would this be any more Life," says Hopkins in the play, "would this be any more Life than a middle-aged lady sitting reading in a garden?" Yes, I'm afraid it would.

SATURDAY, 18 MARCH 1978

London

When I come back from filming, emerge, as Goffman would say, from an intense and prolonged period of social interaction, I feel raw, as if I have in some unspecified way made a fool of myself.

TUESDAY, 11 APRIL 1978

Morecambe: *All Day on the Sands*

A bright, bitter cold morning. Over the sands the low tumbled hills of the Lake District and one white mountain. Blue council buses ferry schoolchildren along the empty promenade. Old couples take the air. Why do people find the seaside out of season sad? I never do. It's much sadder when the streets are filled with tired families, cross because they're not happy. Which is what the film is about.

Two women pass. "I said to him, 'If you've brought me here to mix with a lot of old people, you're mistaken. You've got the bowling green to go to. Well, I'm not spending the rest of my life on bowling greens.' "

An old gentleman watches the filming on the front. Apparently he made boots for Field Marshal Earl Haig. Another front. This information he volunteers readily to anyone who comes near him, so I keep out of his way, suspecting he is a bore. This is foolish, since to be a bore about making boots for Earl Haig constitutes interest. A life flying this small flag. Had he met the Field Marshal?

"Oh, yes."

"What was he like?"

A long pause. "Very smart."

FRIDAY, 14 APRIL 1978

Morecambe: *All Day on the Sands*

Alun Armstrong, who plays the father in the film, is full of jokes and stories and on the go the whole day. This morning he sits apart, silent and withdrawn. I ask him what's the matter.

"I woke up in the night and I'd nothing to read, so picked up my Gideon's, opened it at a page, the way you do, thinking there might be some sort of revelation, change my way of life

21

and so on. And it's Ecclesiastes, 'the joker is a foolish man', 'empty pots make most noise', all that stuff. I mean *my story*. So I'm piping down a bit this morning."

On a wall on one of the roads off the promenade in clear large letters written without haste and correctly spelled: "Mark Lambert is a Paedophiliac (Ask Tracy)".

SUNDAY, 30 APRIL 1978

Hartlepool: *Afternoon Off*

In my mind's eye I had seen this play taking place in Scarborough or Harrogate. It is the story of a Chinese waiter on his afternoon off, searching the town for a girl called Iris, whom he has been told fancies him. I'd got the idea from a Chinese waiter I glimpsed from a car, wandering about a small town on early closing day. That had been in Lewes in 1972. Now it is six years later and it's not Lewes, it's not even Harrogate but somewhere that couldn't be more different, Hartlepool.

It was this main street that gave Stephen the idea of setting the film here. The buildings all date from the same period, around when the town was founded in the 1880s. The date gives it the look of a town in a western, the main street lined with saloons, shipping offices, tackle shops and behind it, like in a western, the desert. Only it's a desert of rubble where all the symmetrical side streets have been demolished, leaving only occasional outcrops of bright, boiled brick, where the grander buildings await a more elaborate and accomplished destruction. A sense too of the proximity of Germany and the Baltic coast. The dullness and loutishness of a rundown port; pubs, prostitutes. Sailors returning.

Sunday morning and the street is closed off, emptied of cars as rails are laid down for the camera. It's Meccano time, a big tracking shot, "real filming". Along the pavement a wavering trail of blood leads the length of the street. Last night a man was stabbed and wandered along, holding his arm, looking for a taxi. Blood is sticky. It smears on the pavement and members of the unit examine it curiously. It does seem indelible, more so than paint. Seagulls yelp over the empty street and mount each other on chimneystacks this grey Sunday while boys in baggy trousers phone possible girls from shattered phone boxes.

MONDAY, I MAY 1978

Hartlepool: *Afternoon Off*

We film in the sluice room of the cottage hospital. Racks of stainless-steel bottles and bedpans, a sink that flushes and a hideously stained drum on which the bedpans are sluiced out. This room would be my mother's nightmare. Conditions are cramped and I crouch behind the camera tripod in order to see the action. I am kneeling on the floor under the bedpan sluice. If my Mam saw this she would want to throw away trousers, raincoat, every particle of clothing that might have been touched and polluted. This has got into the film. Thora Hird plays a patient in the hospital being visited by her husband. "I bet the house is upside down," she says to him.

"It never is," says her husband. "I did the kitchen floor this morning."

"Which bucket did you use?"

"The red one."

She is outraged. "That's the outside bucket. I shall have it all to do again."

I am assuming this is common ground and that the tortuous boundary between the clean and the dirty is a frontier most households share. It was very marked in ours. My mother maintained an intricate hierarchy of cloths, buckets and dusters, to the Byzantine differentiations of which she alone was privy. Some cloths were dish cloths but not sink cloths; some were for the sink but not for the floor. There were dirty buckets and

23

clean buckets, brushes for indoors, brushes for the flags. One mop had a universal application while another had a unique and terrible purpose and had to be kept outside, hung on the wall. And however rinsed and clean these utensils were they remained tainted by their awful function. Left to himself my Dad would violate these taboos, using the first thing that came to hand to clean the hearth or wash the floor. "It's all nowt," he'd mutter, but if Mam was around he knew it saved time and temper to observe her order of things. Latterly, disposable cloths and kitchen rolls tended to blur these ancient distinctions but the basic structure remained, perhaps the firmest part of the framework of her world. When she was ill with depression the order broke down: the house became dirty. Spotless though Dad kept it, she saw it as "upside down", dust an unstemmable tide and the house's (imagined) squalor a talking point for the neighbours. So that when she came home from the hospital, bright and better, her first comment was always how clean the house looked. And not merely the house. It was as if the whole world and her existence in it had been rinsed clean.

Grand Hotel, Hartlepool. Breakfast. The waitresses are two local girls who are marshalled, instructed and generally ordered about by an elderly waitress with jet-black hair and glasses. This morning she is off. A man behind me raises his voice to ask whether anyone is serving his table. The two young waitresses whisper briefly, then one goes across. The man studies the menu.

"I would like fresh grapefruit."

"Are you suffering from diabetes?"

A hush has fallen on the room.

"I beg your pardon?"

The waitress smiles helpfully. "Fresh grapefruit. Are you diabetic?"

The man is now in a towering rage. "No, I am not diabetic. Furthermore I am not suffering from Bell's palsy, tuberculosis, cancer or Parkinson's disease."

Everyone buries themselves in their cornflakes as the waitress, scarlet, rushes from the room to tell the kitchen of this madman.

TUESDAY, 2 MAY 1978

Hartlepool: *Afternoon Off*

I take photographs in the old cemetery by the sea on the north side of the headland. The graveyard is flanked by two huge factories, where the pier of Steetley Magnesite runs out into the sea. The graves are of dead mariners, a Norwegian from a shipwreck, a man killed by a shell in the bombardment of Hartlepool in 1914 and many men and children killed "in the course of their employment".

Filming gives one an oblique perspective on English life, taking one into places one would not otherwise go, bringing one up against people one would never otherwise meet. This morning busmen in the depot on Church Street, yesterday the chef and waiters in the hotel kitchens. I have very little knowledge of "ordinary life". I imagine it in a script and come up against the reality only when the script gets filmed. So the process can be a bit of an eye-opener, a kind of education. Cameramen in particular are educated like this, men of the world who have odd pockets of understanding and experience gleaned from the films they have worked on. I imagine someone could be educated in the same way by promiscuity.

Sunderland. An old-fashioned shoe shop. High ladders and shelves piled with shoeboxes. Feeling this is what a genuine writer would do I make a note of the labels:

> Alabaster Softee Leather
> Clover Trilobel Fur Bound Bootees
> Buffalo Grain Softee Chukkas
> Malt Gibsons

Fawn Suede Apron Casuals
Burnished Brown Concealed Gusset Casuals
Red Derby Nocap
Tan Gibson Bruised Look
Mahogany Lear Peep Toe

WEDNESDAY, 3 MAY 1978

Hartlepool: *Afternoon Off*

We are filming an OAP concert at St Hilda's Church Hall. The
Chinese waiter wanders on to the stage while two entertainers
are giving a rendition of "Pedro the Fisherman" to a whistled
accompaniment of an audience of old ladies. They arrive in a
coach, smart and warm in fur hats, check coats and little bootees
with one solitary man. I see my father in him, going with my
Mam on the W.I. trip from the village. "Well, your Mam and
me always do things together. We don't want splitting up to go
with lots of different folks." And he was not embarrassed by it.

My mother's description of her clothes:
    My other shoes
    My warm boots
    My tweedy coat
    That greeny coat of mine
    That fuzzy blue coat I have
    My coat with the round buttons
Like the inventory of a medieval will.

Casual onlookers find it difficult to detect the hierarchy of a film
unit. Who is in charge? It seems to be the cameraman. He is
making them move all the lights anyway. Or is it one of those
two young men who keep changing their minds about where
everybody in the audience is meant to sit? Perhaps it's the man
with the long microphone. Certainly, now that he's shaken his

head they're changing it all again. The proper actors haven't even appeared yet, you'd think they'd have some say. Suddenly everything settles down and somebody shouts out (quite rudely), "Settle, everybody, settle", and the boss turns out to be the scruffy young man who has been sat on the windowsill doing the crossword. He scarcely looks old enough.

And so it was in the days when Mam and Dad used to come and watch the filming. Dad would think he was talking to a key figure on the film, when in fact he was talking to one of the props boys or the animal handler, members of the unit I'd scarcely come across and whose names I didn't know. Once when they visited me at Oxford they took my scout for a don, and in the theatre my dresser for John Gielgud. And it's happened to me. When we were on Broadway with *Beyond the Fringe* the Kennedys came backstage after the show. Having been introduced I spent most of my time talking to a distinguished but rather abstracted young man who, though (and perhaps because) he kept looking over my shoulder I took to be an important section of the New Frontier. He was a secret serviceman.

SATURDAY, 13 MAY 1978

Hartlepool: *Afternoon Off*

The final sequences with Peter Postlethwaite and Stan Richards, in the Municipal Art Gallery and Museum, which combines art, archaeology, natural and local history. Downstage is an exhibition of flower arrangements, "Britain in Bloom", with the comments of the adjudicators affixed: "It speaks to me"; "Lovely arrangement, but a bit delicate flowerwise". Upstairs a case of stuffed birds and in another case, "Hartlepool in Palaeolithic Times". There is an old bicycle, a Japanese suit of armour and a dismal collection of pictures, scarcely above the highland-cattle level. Kids wander through, bored out of their

27

heads, mystified by a culture that can comprehend a Japanese suit of armour, a stuffed otter and a calcified Roman waterpipe.

The filming finishes as filming usually does, with a wild track. In the midst of clearing up everybody suddenly freezes into silence and immobility as on sound only the actors record their lines.

ME, I'M AFRAID OF
VIRGINIA WOOLF

CHARACTERS

NARRATOR
HOPKINS
GINGER-HAIRED GIRL
DOCTOR
WILLARD
CONDUCTRESS
LARGE BLACK LADY
MRS HOPKINS
WENDY
MRS BROADBENT
MRS TUCKER
MISS GIBBONS
SKINNER
MR DODDS
MRS GARLAND
MAUREEN
TRICKETT
BOY IN TRICKETT'S CLASS
ANOTHER BOY IN TRICKETT'S CLASS
BOSWELL
WOMAN IN WENDY'S CLASS
CARETAKER
MAN IN LAVATORY
BOY ON BUS
GIRL ON BUS
CONDUCTOR
WOMAN AT INFIRMARY
APPRENTICES, YOGA LADIES, INFIRMARY PATIENTS
BUS PASSENGERS, etc.

Me, I'm Afraid of Virginia Woolf was first transmitted by London Weekend Television on 2 December 1978. The cast included:

NARRATOR	Alan Bennett
HOPKINS	Neville Smith
GINGER-HAIRED GIRL	Julie Walters
DOCTOR	Frank Middlemass
WILLARD	Robert Longdon
MRS HOPKINS	Thora Hird
WENDY	Carol Macready
MRS BROADBENT	Margaret Courtenay
MRS TUCKER	Lynne Carol
MISS GIBBONS	Barbara Hicks
SKINNER	Derek Thompson
MR DODDS	Hugh Lloyd
MRS GARLAND	Gillian Martell
MAUREEN	Janine Duvitski
TRICKETT	Bernard Wrigley
BOY IN TRICKETT'S CLASS	Paul Rosebury
ANOTHER BOY IN TRICKETT'S CLASS	Bernard Strother
BOSWELL	Alan Igbon
WOMAN IN WENDY'S CLASS	Pat Beckett
CARETAKER	Dickie Arnold
Producer and Director	Stephen Frears
Designer	Martin Johnson
Music	George Fenton

PART ONE

1. INT. DOCTOR'S WAITING ROOM. DAY
The waiting room is full and the first sequence is on the faces of patients waiting, the bell ringing and one patient going into the surgery as another comes out. HOPKINS, *a man of about 35, enters the waiting room.*

NARRATOR: (*Voice over*) Hopkins, coming into the waiting room, found only one seat vacant, next to a girl with gingerish hair. He sat down. Time passed. The room emptied. And soon there was only Hopkins marooned beside the ginger-haired girl.
(HOPKINS *is reading and looking uncomfortable.*)
(*Voice over*) Hopkins's problem was this:
there were now so many empty seats that if he went on sitting there the girl would think he wanted to sit next to her. But if he sat somewhere else she would think he didn't. Life, it seemed to Hopkins, was full of such problems and literature was not much help.
(HOPKINS *shuts his book. Gets up. Looks, rather stagily, at a magazine and sits down again one seat away from his previous seat, and so from the* GINGER-HAIRED GIRL.)
HOPKINS: Spread ourselves.
GINGER-HAIRED GIRL: What?
HOPKINS: No need to bunch up. Take your pick.
(*He gets up again and sits somewhere else, even farther off. Spreads his arms across the adjacent chairs, expansively. Then he goes back to his book. Pause.*)
GINGER-HAIRED GIRL: I'm before you!
HOPKINS: I know.
(*Pause.*)

33

GINGER-HAIRED GIRL: They've sent my sputum to Newcastle.
  (*Pause.*)
HOPKINS: Newcastle? What for?
GINGER-HAIRED GIRL: These tests.
HOPKINS: It seems a long way.
GINGER-HAIRED GIRL: Well, they do that now. It's all this
  decentralization. Underdeveloped areas. Light industry.
  The bogey of unemployment. (*Pause.*) It's not a place I've
  been to personally, Newcastle. I've never fancied it
  somehow. Have you been?
HOPKINS: Newcastle? No.
NARRATOR: (*Voice over*) This was a lie. Hopkins had been to
  Newcastle, many times. So why did he not say so? This was
  what he had come to ask the doctor.
HOPKINS: No, I've never been to Newcastle. Nor want to. I've
  never been anywhere up there. Never been to
  Middlesbrough. Sunderland.
GINGER-HAIRED GIRL: (*Scornfully*) You haven't been to
  Sunderland? You've never been to Sunderland? Well, stroll
  on. I've got a sister-in-law lives in Sunderland. I must have
  been there fifty times. Don't try telling me anything about
  Sunderland.
  (*The bell rings and she goes into the surgery.*)
HOPKINS: I'm always doing that. Putting myself in people's
  place. Well, I'm going to cut it out.
  (*Time passes. The* GINGER-HAIRED GIRL *comes out of the
  surgery.*)
  Listen. You know I said I'd never been to Newcastle? Well,
  I have been. I've just remembered. I've been there in fact
  on at least twenty-seven separate occasions.
  (*The* GINGER-HAIRED GIRL *has completely collapsed. She is
  on the verge of tears.* HOPKINS *is abashed.*)
GINGER-HAIRED GIRL: He's sending me to a specialist. I've got
  to go to a specialist.
  (*She exits, leaving* HOPKINS *mortified.*)

2. INT. DOCTOR'S SURGERY. DAY

DOCTOR: Come in, Mr Hopkins, sit down. You notice that we have an alien presence. This is Mr Willard. Mr Willard is a medical student sitting in on my surgery. We're just initiating him into the horrors of general practice, ha ha. Eh, Mr Willard?

(MR WILLARD *is an expressionless youth with a pageboy hair cut.*)

I take it you don't have any objections to him just . . . sitting . . . there. And of course if you did you wouldn't dare say so, I know. Ha ha. Now. (*He has got Hopkins's notes.*) Mr Hopkins has been my patient now for some time . . . let's see . . . two years?

HOPKINS: Two.

DOCTOR: (*Reading rapidly from notes*) Two years. And in that time he's made fairly frequent visits to the surgery with a variety of complaints . . . I see here you first came along complaining of tightness in the chest. Chest and heart subsequently examined, quite sound. Then discomfort in the abdomen, sense of . . . fullness. Our old friend migraine. Even complained of pain . . . ha ha . . . in the neck but again without discernible physical origin. Pain, in short in various departments, though never anything we could quite put our fingers on and I think we more or less decided last time, didn't we, that Mr Hopkins's problem is ah . . . psychological . . . even psychosomatic. None the less real for all that but mental rather than physical. Mr Hopkins is a lecturer at the Polytechnic in Economics.

HOPKINS: English Literature.

DOCTOR: English Literature. Our priceless heritage. I can just about get as far as Agatha Christie. Time, that's the problem. Where do you find it? He has no financial worries. One of those fortunate mortals who are tied to the cost of living and indeed index-linked. He should be laughing . . . but quite plainly isn't. Now why? Mr

Willard, any thoughts?

(WILLARD *remains expressionless, then says something in an undertone to the* DOCTOR.)

Yes. Yes. Mr Willard with the outspokenness of youth, wonders if this is a . . . ah . . . sexual problem. But I'm afraid he scores no points there, does he, Mr Hopkins? Mr Hopkins and I went into all that pretty thoroughly and it appears that while he is not married, wise man, Mr Hopkins has a lady friend with whom he gets on, if not like a house on fire, certainly . . .

HOPKINS: Quite well.

DOCTOR: Not famously, but quite well. No worries at work, no worries at home. How would you sum up your situation, Mr Hopkins?

HOPKINS: I'm not happy. I'm uneasy, uncertain of myself. People make me uneasy.

DOCTOR: Do I make you uneasy?

(HOPKINS *is silent*.)

Does Mr Willard make you uneasy?

HOPKINS: (*Voice over*) Yes. (*Aloud*) No.

DOCTOR: Well, I'm surprised to hear it because he scares the pinstripes off me. Another one of these bright young devils they send us from medical school, Hopkins. Computer diagnosis, tissue type. Brain scan. Technicians, Hopkins, scientists. Run rings round an old quack like me. Me, I just listen and look. Prehistoric.

HOPKINS: I don't feel the same as everybody else.

DOCTOR: We none of us are the same, are we? You, me, Mr Willard.

HOPKINS: I'm always wondering about what people think. That's not healthy, is it?

DOCTOR: It is up to a point.

HOPKINS: I'm not ill. I've got a good job. Should I be happy? I don't know.

DOCTOR: Which of us is happy? I'm not. I don't think friend

Willard is happy.

WILLARD: (*Expressionlessly*) I am, quite.

(*The* DOCTOR *looks intensely disapproving.*)

DOCTOR: I think we'll try you on a different anti-depressant.

Hopkins has gone. The DOCTOR *and* WILLARD *are finishing for the day.*

DOCTOR: Willard. You are young. But in this matter of happiness it has been my experience that we none of us wish to be told of the happiness of others. It does not help, Willard. Confess to misery, say one's life is futile, hail the onset of bankruptcy, yes, Willard, because nothing encourages one's fellows more. They go away smiling. But say, "I am happy. I am having a good time." No, Willard. The spirit plummets. (*Pause.*) What is your chosen field in medicine? Your speciality.

WILLARD: The inner ear.

DOCTOR: Good. Good.

3. INT. BUS. DAY

HOPKINS *gets on the bus. He sits on the seat nearest the platform, so that he is facing the seat opposite, on which is an expressionless* MAN.

NARRATOR: (*Voice over*) Hopkins was never without a book. It wasn't that he was particularly fond of reading; he just liked to have somewhere to look.

(*We see* HOPKINS *avoid the gaze of the man by opening his book. The* CONDUCTRESS *waits for his fare.*)

CONDUCTRESS: What's your book, love?

(HOPKINS *shows it to her as she gives him his ticket.*)

Any good?

HOPKINS: Not really.

CONDUCTRESS: You can't win 'em all.

(*The bus has stopped and a* GIRL *has got on. She sits opposite* HOPKINS.)

NARRATOR: (*Voice over*) A book makes you safe. Shows you're

not out to pick anybody up. Try it on. With a book you're
harmless. Though Hopkins was harmless without a book.

HOPKINS: (*Aloud*) I know.

(*The* GIRL *opposite sees him speak and smiles.*)

NARRATOR: (*Voice over*) Now she thinks he's talking to himself.
(HOPKINS *therefore smiles apologetically at her.*)
(*Voice over*) Now she thinks he's trying to pick her up.
(*The* GIRL *should be slightly amused so that we know, as he
doesn't, that it wouldn't matter if he were.*)

HOPKINS: I wasn't smiling at you. I was actually just smiling at
my book. I've just got to a really funny bit. (*Forces a laugh.*)
It's hysterical.

CONDUCTRESS: Is it fiction or non-fiction?

HOPKINS: Virginia Woolf.

CONDUCTRESS: Is she funny?

HOPKINS: Killing.

(*The* GIRL *gets off and a* LARGE BLACK LADY *gets on and sits
next to* HOPKINS *so that he involuntarily moves a bit to give
her room. Shot of* HOPKINS's *anxious face with his large black
neighbour.*)

I was just thinking: when I made room for you on the seat,
did you notice, I sort of shifted, budged up a bit. Well, that
was all I was doing, making room for you. I mean, I wasn't
moving away because you were bla. . . I'd have done the
same for anybody, that's what I mean. I was just giving you
more room.

LARGE BLACK LADY: What's troublin' you there, man?

HOPKINS: Nothing. Never mind.

4. EXT./INT. STREETS/INSTITUTE. DAY

Cut to either external shot of HOPKINS *walking through the streets
towards the Mechanics Institute or in the building itself. On his way
along corridors towards the municipal cafeteria.*

HOPKINS: (*Voice over*) Why bother what other people think? I
mean. Why bother? (*Aloud*) I am not going to bother.

(*Someone passing looks sharply.*)
(*Voice over*) Now he thinks I'm talking to myself. (*Aloud*)
My God.
(*Someone else looks.*)
(*Voice over*) Now she does too. What's the matter with me?

5. INT. MUNICIPAL CAFETERIA. DAY
HOPKINS *is just sitting down at a table where his* MOTHER *is already firmly installed.*

MRS HOPKINS: You want to be like me. I never bother what
anybody thinks. You're shy. That's your trouble. You take
after me.

HOPKINS: What are you doing here?

MRS HOPKINS: Is it a crime? To want to see one's own flesh and
blood once in a blue moon? Is that a felony? A distant
glimpse of one's only son.

HOPKINS: I've got a class in a minute.

MRS HOPKINS: "College lecturer spurns mother." "I skimped
to give him his start." I know this. You eat the wrong food.
(*Takes one of his chips.*) I don't wonder you're constipated.
Are you constipated?

HOPKINS: No.

MRS HOPKINS: Well, I would be. Eating that muck. Mind you,
my stomach's on a knife edge. The doctor said, "Mrs
Hopkins. It could just go either way." (*Pause.*) When did
you last go?

HOPKINS: I am not constipated.

(*A* WOMAN *at the next table looks.*)

MRS HOPKINS: That's right. Show me up. I'm only your mother.

HOPKINS: What do you want to be coming down here for?

MRS HOPKINS: Because I'm daft, that's why. Because I want my
head examining. They've given you a cracked cup. Let's
take it back.

HOPKINS: No.

MRS HOPKINS: I thought that was the latest thing with you

39

people now, the consumer. You've got to stand up for yourself in this take-it-or-leave-it society. Drink out of the other side then.

HOPKINS: What're you frightened of me catching? VD?

(*The* WOMAN *looks again.*)

MRS HOPKINS: Do you want to humiliate me?

HOPKINS: What've you come down here for? What do you want to see me about?

MRS HOPKINS: What do I want to see you about? Do I have to want to see you about something? I want to see you about having brought you up single-handed. I want to see you about having put you in for a scholarship. I want to see you about being my son.

(*Pause.*)

HOPKINS: Oh, Mam.

MRS HOPKINS: Is that her?

HOPKINS: Who?

MRS HOPKINS: Your girlfriend.

HOPKINS: I haven't got a girlfriend.

MRS HOPKINS: Who was it Mrs Goodall saw you with?

HOPKINS: She's a girl. She's a friend. She's not a girlfriend. Mrs Goodall.

MRS HOPKINS: I don't know why you patronize this place. They don't even run to a toasted teacake. I said, "I want a toasted teacake." She said did I mean a cheeseburger! Yorkshire! It's the home of toasted teacake. You shouldn't have to spell it out. It's barbarism. And it's not clean. Look at that sauce-bottle top. It's a Mecca for germs. You'd think they could run to a dispenser. Hygiene's just gone out of the window. Before you came in I paid a visit: that toilet's a real hell-hole.

NARRATOR: (*Optional; voice over*) Life for Hopkins's mother was a canopy slung between three poles. Dirt, Disease and the Lavatory.

HOPKINS: Mam, can I ask you something? Why did you call me

Trevor? You christened me Trevor. Why?

MRS HOPKINS: After thirty-five years you ask me why we called you Trevor.

HOPKINS: Well, why?

MRS HOPKINS: Because your Dad and me chose it. Because it's a nice name.

HOPKINS: Well, I hate it. I hate my name. I think maybe that's what's wrong with me. Being called Trevor. I'm not a Trevor, am I? Couldn't you see that?

MRS HOPKINS: At six weeks old?

HOPKINS: I'm a James or a Charles. A Martin even. But not Trevor.

MRS HOPKINS: You're our Trevor.

NARRATOR: (*Voice over*) Trevor was what he was called. Trevor was not what he was. In the entire history of the world Hopkins could recall no one of note who had been called Trevor.

HOPKINS: You're in the outside lane before even the pistol goes. It's not Trevor Proust, is it? Trevor Strachey. Trevor Sibelius. Lenin, Stalin, where would they be if they'd been called Trevor?

MRS HOPKINS: What about Mrs Beaver's son? He's called Trevor and he's the North-western Area Manager for Kayser Bondor. Trevor hasn't stopped him getting to the top. Trevor.

HOPKINS: Don't keep on saying it.

MRS HOPKINS: (*Looking at the evening paper*) Blaming your name. What if you were called Doris? I am. I see the President of Romania's mother's died. There's always trouble for somebody. How's your work going?

HOPKINS: All right.

MRS HOPKINS: "All right."

HOPKINS: Well, you wouldn't understand if I told you.

MRS HOPKINS: I might. You underestimate your mother.

HOPKINS: Well, I'll tell you. I'm working on an article on

"Culture and Expropriation in the Novels of E. M. Forster".

(*Long long pause.*)

MRS HOPKINS: That woman's just put a sandwich in her handbag. And she's got a fur coat on. I'd have been educated if I could have stopped on at school. The teacher always read out my compositions. You get it all from me. Your Dad never opened a book in his life. Bless him.

HOPKINS: I'll have to go in a minute.

MRS HOPKINS: I just wish it wasn't called polytechnic. Why don't they call it a university? I tell folks you're at the polytechnic and they think you teach woodwork.

NARRATOR: (*Voice over*) Not married at 35 and sat here with his mam. What did it look like? Hopkins knew only too well what it looked like.

(*A* WOMAN *coming in gives him a little wave, instantly spotted by* MRS HOPKINS, *then goes and queues at the cafeteria.*)

MRS HOPKINS: Oh. Is that her?

HOPKINS: Where?

MRS HOPKINS: Where! The one who's waving at you. *Wave.*

(*He waves half-heartedly and* MRS HOPKINS *smiles graciously.*)

How old is she?

HOPKINS: I don't know. Thirty.

MRS HOPKINS: Is that what she says? Mrs Goodall said she was oldish.

HOPKINS: Are you satisfied now, now you've seen her?

MRS HOPKINS: I had some purchases to make and I was in the vicinity. What's her name? Shirley?

HOPKINS: Wendy.

MRS HOPKINS: Same thing. Why hasn't she got off before now?

HOPKINS: Maybe she doesn't want to.

MRS HOPKINS: They all want to. Every woman wants to. Unless they get thwarted. There'll be something about her else why's she wasting her time teaching yogi. I know one thing.

She shouldn't wear trousers.

HOPKINS: Who?

MRS HOPKINS: Your girl.

HOPKINS: She's not "my girl". I don't have a girl. She's just
somebody I . . .

MRS HOPKINS: Somebody you what?

HOPKINS: Somebody I know.

MRS HOPKINS: Yes. I know too. Somebody you carry on with.

HOPKINS: Mam, I'm 35.

MRS HOPKINS: Don't tell me. By the time I was 35 I was
married and two children.

HOPKINS: Anyway, they're not trousers. They're ski pants.

MRS HOPKINS: Oh, ski pants, is it now? (*Pause.*) She's not one
of these lesbians, is she?

HOPKINS: What do you know about lesbians?

MRS HOPKINS: You'd be surprised what I know. More in my
head than nits. There was a talk on them on *Women's Hour*.
I can't see what folks make such a fuss about. It's only
women and other women. Like me and Mrs Goodall.

HOPKINS: You and Mrs Goodall?

MRS HOPKINS: Friends. Doing things together.

HOPKINS: Doing what together?

MRS HOPKINS: Having tea in Marshall and Snelgrove's.

HOPKINS: Having tea in Marshall and Snelgrove's isn't
lesbianism.

MRS HOPKINS: It's only liking being with other women.

HOPKINS: Not in Marshall and Snelgrove.

MRS HOPKINS: Well, where?

HOPKINS: Bed.

(*Long outraged pause.*)

You brought the subject up.

MRS HOPKINS: Well? So. Anyway I've been in bed with other
women.

HOPKINS: Who?

MRS HOPKINS: Your Aunty Phyllis for a start.

HOPKINS: Aunty Phyllis isn't women. Anyway, when were you in bed with Aunty Phyllis?

MRS HOPKINS: During the air raids. When Uncle Bernard was in North Africa.

HOPKINS: Where was my Dad?

MRS HOPKINS: On nights.

HOPKINS: That's not lesbianism.

MRS HOPKINS: It wasn't for me. It might have been for her.

HOPKINS: What did she say it was?

MRS HOPKINS: Nerves. Anyroads you seem to know a lot about it.

HOPKINS: Lesbianism? Yes, well I come across it in literature.

MRS HOPKINS: Well, I hope it is in literature and not in Huddersfield. Course it's all right if you're educated. That makes it all *carte blanche*. Well, I was the one that wanted you educated. You want to remember that when you're running your mother down.

HOPKINS: I don't.

MRS HOPKINS: You're not, are you?

HOPKINS: What?

MRS HOPKINS: That.

HOPKINS: Lesbian?

MRS HOPKINS: No. The other.

HOPKINS: Mam. I'm nothing, Mam.

MRS HOPKINS: I bet they've never seen Zermatt.

HOPKINS: What?

MRS HOPKINS: Them ski pants. I see Mrs Proctor in them sometimes and she's got a bum like a boiler end. Oh. She's sitting somewhere else.

(WENDY *has sat down at another table*.)

I can't be good enough for her.

HOPKINS: Mam.

MRS HOPKINS: No. I'm going now. I know when I'm not wanted.

HOPKINS: Mam. It's all right. Stay.

MRS HOPKINS: No. You have your own young lives to lead.

HOPKINS: Mam.

MRS HOPKINS: Give us a kiss.

(*He lets himself be kissed.*)

Oh, I've lipsticked you.

(*She rubs the mark off with her hanky, then goes.*)

NARRATOR: (*Voice over*) Mrs Hopkins had it in mind to pause, for a second, by Wendy's table in order to give her a smile of infinite pain and resignation. A smile which would say, "Be gentle with him, Wendy. I am his mother." But Wendy was busy rubbing a bit of yoghurt off her blouse and so the moment passed.

(WENDY *comes over with her muesli and slopping cup of coffee.*)

WENDY: I couldn't have sat with you, Trevor. I wanted to, but I couldn't. Mother and son. You made such a nice picture. So complete somehow. And such a good, good face, Trevor. It shines out.

HOPKINS: You've got yoghurt on your chin.

WENDY: Trevor.

NARRATOR: (*Voice over*) Hating his name, Hopkins had found someone who said it 103 times.

WENDY: What was she saying?

HOPKINS: Mam? She was just telling me how my Aunty Phyllis and her had this lesbian relationship.

WENDY: Trevor. How wonderful. And how wonderful she was able to tell you. You must be very close. It's sad how those nearest to us are in some sense the furthest away. How we see them as *parents*. Mother, capital M. Father, capital F. Not people.

HOPKINS: Small p.

WENDY: Exactly. And whereas you and I probably assume that so-called deviant relationships are confined to the more intellectual sections of society, there is no reason why they shouldn't occur lower down the social scale where people are more instinctual.

HOPKINS: Your hair's in your muesli.

(WENDY *extracts it and puts her hair in her mouth and sucks the muesli from her hair*.)

WENDY: How did it happen?

HOPKINS: They slept together during an air raid and soon they had this relationship roaring along. You know how it is.

WENDY: Isn't that marvellous?

HOPKINS: I found it all rather sordid.

WENDY: No. No, Trevor, it's marvellous.

HOPKINS: It's five to seven.

WENDY: Trevor, can I tell you something very seriously? You eat the wrong food. I was reading the other day they've done a study of dandruff and do you know what they've traced it back to?

HOPKINS: Masturbation?

WENDY: Fried foods.

(*They get up to go,* WENDY *probably spilling something else in the process*.)

And as fried foods are the culprit in heart disease as well, it's only a short step to realizing that dandruff may be an early warning sign of heart attacks. Nature has a language, you see, if only we'd learn to read it.

6. INT. HOPKINS'S CLASSROOM. EVENING

Half a dozen people, mainly in their fifties and sixties, are sitting, waiting.

MRS BROADBENT: (*A big masterful woman*) Late again!

MRS TUCKER: (*A small vindictive one*) He'll be with that slut from Transcendental Meditation. Having a little tête-à-tête.

MRS BROADBENT: In the Corporation's time.

MRS TUCKER: Of course.

MRS BROADBENT: It all comes out of the rates.

MISS GIBBONS: (*A more sympathetic figure*) I see she's brought him his flower again.

(MAUREEN, *a wet-looking girl, comes in with a carnation which she puts in a vase on the desk. She cleans the blackboard and gets Hopkins's desk ready.*)

MRS TUCKER: His mother goes to my chiropodist. Smartish-looking woman, pointed glasses, has a fawny Raglan coat. What is it this week?

MISS GIBBONS: A carnation.

MRS TUCKER: She has quite a nice little semi up at Lawnswood. It was a rose last week. Slipping.

MISS GIBBONS: Sir Malcolm Sargent used to have that.

MRS TUCKER: What?

MISS GIBBONS: Every day of his life. A single blood-red carnation. Didn't matter where he was. Bridlington. Buenos Aires. Six o'clock. Pageboy. Knock, knock. "Sir Malcolm, your carnation."

MRS TUCKER: And who was it?

MISS GIBBONS: He never knew. A Mystery Woman.

MRS TUCKER: Save him a lot of money. Carnations are wicked. She'd send it through Interpol.

MRS BROADBENT: Multiply this on a national scale and you can see why they're so sceptical at the World Bank. Why should they bail us out? He's seven minutes late.

MRS TUCKER: He wouldn't be late if we were in West Germany.
(MAUREEN *has started to put up a large photograph. She half unrolls it, then rolls it up hurriedly again and sits down.*)
She's not put up the photographs. Maureen. The photographs, love. Are you not putting up the photographs?
(MAUREEN *shakes her head and won't look round. They look at each other in wild surmise.*)

7. INT. INSTITUTE CORRIDOR. EVENING
HOPKINS *and* WENDY *are walking down a corridor in the Mechanics Institute.*
HOPKINS: Am I coming back tonight?

WENDY: Do you want to?

HOPKINS: That's why I'm saying, "Am I coming back tonight?" I wouldn't say that if I didn't want to, would I?

WENDY: You might. I get the feeling you don't really want to. I get the feeling it's not me you really want. Not the real me, anyway.

(*Lounging in the corridor outside the classroom is* SKINNER, *a relaxed and good-looking young man.*)

SKINNER: Sir's late.

HOPKINS: I'll be right with you. Am I coming back tonight?

WENDY: Come if you want to. If you really want to. And it is the real me. The real you wanting the real me. Trevor.

HOPKINS: Oh God.

SKINNER: Five past, sir.

HOPKINS: I'll be right with you.

WENDY: You see, it's not what we do, it's the relationship that matters. I feel anyway.

HOPKINS: This is Mr Skinner from my class.

SKINNER: Dave, sir.

HOPKINS: This is Miss Turnbull.

SKINNER: I know. From judo.

WENDY: Yoga. I'm late. I don't know, Trevor. I'm doing deep meditation with my class tonight and when I go under I sometimes come out feeling completely different. Sometimes when I come out I feel it's all irrelevant.

HOPKINS: What?

WENDY: Sex.

MRS BROADBENT: (*Overhearing*) Mr Hopkins. You are late.

8. INT. HOPKINS'S CLASSROOM. EVENING

The main speaking members of the class are MRS BROADBENT, MRS TUCKER, MISS GIBBONS *and* MAUREEN, *whom we have already seen;* MRS GARLAND, *a rather arty woman;* MR DODDS, *a cantankerous self-taught man of about 60, and* SKINNER, *who is about 25.*

HOPKINS: I'm going to talk tonight about that group of writers, painters and . . . friends . . . that we call the Bloomsbury Group. In particular I am going to talk about two novelists, E. M. Forster and Virginia Woolf. (*He turns to the blackboard and writes up their names.*) E. M. Forster. Virginia Woolf.

(*While his back is turned* MRS TUCKER *is gesturing to* MAUREEN *to pin up the posters.* MAUREEN *won't take any notice.*)

Maureen. Did you not put up the photographs this week?

MRS TUCKER: I told her.

HOPKINS: Maureen.

(HOPKINS *shrugs and does it himself. He unrolls the picture of E. M. Forster. It has a moustache drawn on it, a little beard and a large cigar. He unrolls the picture of Virginia Woolf. This has been decorated with a large pair of tits.*)

PART TWO

9. INT. HOPKINS'S CLASSROOM. EVENING

MRS TUCKER: It's shocking.

MISS GIBBONS: Wicked.

MR DODDS: Wicked? It's bloody blasphemy.

HOPKINS: Well. I'm sure he wouldn't have minded (*Meaning Forster*). Why should we?

MRS BROADBENT: Why should we? The point is: these photographs are Council property.

(MAUREEN *is busy trying to rub out the decorations on the photographs.*)

MR DODDS: They want horsewhipping. They want taking out and horsewhipping.

HOPKINS: It's only a joke, probably.

MRS BROADBENT: A joke? Is twopence on the rates a joke? Because that's what this sort of thing is costing the local authority. Leaving aside social workers, family service units and all that paraphernalia. A joke is it? Oh. Ha ha.

MR DODDS: They want taking out publicly, their trousers taken down and horsewhipping.

MAUREEN: Mr Hopkins. Could I borrow a bit of your carnation water?

(*She tries to wash the lines off.*)

HOPKINS: Never mind, Maureen.

MRS TUCKER: Do you know what I blame? These felt-tip pens.

SKINNER: Yeah. We should have stuck to stone tablets.

MRS TUCKER: Them aerosol things. It only takes a couple of squirts. Squirt, squirt, and it's an obscenity.

SKINNER: Squirt, squirt.

MRS TUCKER: You stand in the bus shelter and you don't know where to look.

MISS GIBBONS: You see all sorts written up in lifts nowadays. I saw a shocking word in Boots.

MR DODDS: They want bringing out, their trousers taking down and, in front of assembled civic and religious dignitaries and leaders of community groups, horsewhipping.

HOPKINS: Leave it, Maureen.

MISS GIBBONS: They vandalized my kiosk.

MRS BROADBENT: The Parks Department lay out thousands in geraniums alone.

MRS TUCKER: And just try and spend a penny in Horsforth. You can go for miles and not find a single viable toilet.

MR DODDS: And when they've been horsewhipped they want parading through the streets to the new complex and made to stand up and apologize for what they've done. They should then have to spend every Saturday doing voluntary work for pensioners and disabled people and then periodically be horsewhipped again.

MRS GARLAND: We must look deeper. It's all this urban decay. The inner cities.

SKINNER: And her titties.

MRS GARLAND: I feel sorry for them, I do.

MRS BROADBENT: I don't.

MRS GARLAND: I pity them. Finding breasts funny. Are breasts funny? Not in my book. Breasts are beautiful.

SKINNER: Seconded.

MRS BROADBENT: I prefer the singular. Bust.

MRS GARLAND: Why? Bust is such an ugly word. Hard. Unyielding. Bust. Virginia Woolf's bust. No. Breasts. Breast is such a beautiful word. The sound of it. Feel it in your mouth: breast, breast, breast. Say it everybody. Soft and restful. Nothing to be ashamed of. We all have them. (MAUREEN *looks up, since she plainly hasn't, and goes back to her erasing.*)

MAUREEN: I think I may be able to get his cigar off.

HOPKINS: It doesn't *matter*. Maureen.

SKINNER: Sir. Sir.

HOPKINS: Yes, Skinner.

SKINNER: Dave, sir. You sir, me Dave.

MRS BROADBENT: Why should he call you Dave? He doesn't call me Pauline.

MRS TUCKER: Is that your name?

MRS BROADBENT: Yes. Why?

MRS TUCKER: Nothing. Mine's Beryl.

MISS GIBBONS: Our Gillian has a guinea-pig called Beryl.
(*This gets her a look from* MRS TUCKER.)

HOPKINS: You were saying, Skinner?

SKINNER: I reckon our Phantom Scribbler is indulging in a crude form of literary criticism. This basically is a guy who is trying in his simple peasant way to say that the novels of the lady and gentleman in question are deficient in some vital particular.

HOPKINS: Hit us again . . . Dave.

SKINNER: Take the novels of the lady in question, Virginia Woolf. Sensitive, yes. Poetic, yes. Gutsy? No.

HOPKINS: No.

SKINNER: And similarly friend Forster.

MRS GARLAND: I love Forster.

SKINNER: I know, dear, but he wasn't exactly Clint Eastwood, was he?

NARRATOR: (*Voice over*) Skinner was wearing an ear-ring. Hopkins longed to wear an ear-ring but he knew he could never carry it off. Skinner carried it off beautifully. Hopkins hated Skinner and longed to be him.

HOPKINS: Well, what do we think of this point Mr Skinner has made? Anybody? Perhaps instead of feeling outraged and somehow . . . got at, we should use that outrage as a jumping-off point for a discussion of whether these elements, symbolized by the breasts, the moustache and the large cigar are what our two authors lack.

MRS BROADBENT: And what about the perpetrators? I suppose

we discuss it with them too.

SKINNER: Yeah, why not?

MRS TUCKER: It's them youths from the Trigonometry class. They're always in and out, they're the culprits.

HOPKINS: I don't think it's important, is it?

MRS BROADBENT: Some of us may not have had a university education, Mr Hopkins, but we can teach you a lesson in civic responsibility. If you won't go into the Trigonometry class, I shall.

MAUREEN: Please, Mr Hopkins. I've rubbed her nose off.

(MAUREEN *holds up the photograph of Virginia Woolf minus the nose.*)

10. INT. TRICKETT'S CLASSROOM. EVENING

The Mechanical Drawing class, in contrast to the class in Comparative Literature, is very full. Apprentices, 18-year-olds, about a third of them white, the rest Asian or West Indian. They are being addressed by MR TRICKETT, *a rat. He is at the blackboard.*

TRICKETT: Page seventeen of your Yarwood. To construct an equilateral triangle given side lengths AB equals BC equals CA equals 75 millimetres. First job anybody?

BOY: Draw AB, sir.

(HOPKINS *enters with the mutilated photograph rolled up.*)

TRICKETT: Draw AB, sir. (*Does so.*) Job number two?

ANOTHER BOY: Set compasses to 75 millimetres.

TRICKETT: Set compasses to 75 millimetres. Having set compasses where do I put them? And wipe that smile off your coal-black jib, Boswell. Where do I put them? I put them where page seventeen of your Yarwood tells me I put them.

BOSWELL: Centre A and B, sir.

TRICKETT: Centre A and B. Cease your labours for one moment, friends. I spy strangers. Be seated, Boswell. A denizen from the lofty spheres of literature has deigned to grace our humble classroom. Señor Hopkins, what can we do for

you? The isosceles triangle, is it? The square on the
hypotenuse? I'll come down there to you in a minute, lad.

BOY: He's got my T-square, sir.

TRICKETT: If I come down there I'll have more than your T-
square. Now then, Hopkins.

(HOPKINS *unrolls the photograph so that only* TRICKETT *can
see it.*)

HOPKINS: I wondered whether any of your class did this.

TRICKETT: Oh dear, oh dear, oh dear. Oh dear. Now, lads. Mr
Hopkins would like to know whether there is an artist in
our midst. Some student of the female anatomy has been
embellishing Mr Hopkins's visual aids.

(*He shows the picture to the class. Great glee. Shining, black
glee.*)

Right. Stand up the Michelangelo. Look at them, Hopkins.
Regardez. Innocence written in every cloddish
unenlightened line of their features. Draw? This lot? They
can hardly hold a pen. Who is the lady in question?

HOPKINS: Virginia Woolf.

TRICKETT: Virginia Woolf. Virginia Woolf, friends.

BOSWELL: Who is she, sir?

TRICKETT: Tell us, Hopkins. Expound.

HOPKINS: She's a novelist.

TRICKETT: She is a novelist, Boswell.

BOSWELL: Gormless-looking cow.

TRICKETT: Boswell thinks she is a gormless-looking cow. A
gormless-looking cow, Boswell, is that what you think?

BOSWELL: Yes, sir.

TRICKETT: Well, don't. Do you understand me. Why? Because,
friend Boswell, that is lip. L–I–P. Lip.

BOSWELL: Sometimes it's lip and sometimes it's not lip. I never
know.

TRICKETT: Exactly, Boswell, exactly. However. You know my
class, Hopkins. Deprived products of broken homes,
condemned to labour out their days at ordinary common

repetitive tasks. Even the best of them are factory
fodder, Hopkins. What are you, Boswell?

BOSWELL: Factory fodder, sir.

TRICKETT: Exactly. If you are lucky. And the rest, Hopkins,
Y.U.P.s. Have you come across yups yet? These are they.
Young unemployed persons, the latest underprivileged group
to be clasped to the dry bosom of the Welfare State. Creatures
sunk in the trough of ignorance, lasciviousness, foolishness
and despair. And from which there is one thing and one thing
only that can deliver them, Hopkins. Literature, Hopkins?
No. Virginia Woolf? No. Art? No. The one thing that will
deliver them is their Higher National Certificate. But we shall
not achieve it like this, my friend. Goodnight.

(*He pushes* HOPKINS *out into the corridor.*)

11. INT. WENDY'S CLASSROOM. EVENING

WENDY'S *Yoga class. The class is in full swing, which is to say
everyone is motionless, involved in some contemplative exercise.*

WENDY: Let your skeleton grow heavy but your body light.
Take the left side of your face to the left. Take the right
side of your face to the right. Take the back of your head to
the front of your head. And, in your own time . . . let the
silence in. Let your eyes become heavy. Slowly open your
eyes and let the peace in.

(*A* WOMAN *opens her eyes not to let the peace in but to watch* MRS
BROADBENT *and* HOPKINS *who have come in with the damaged
poster. She gives them a shy, embarrassed smile. Almost a wink.*)
Open your eyes to the utmost. Open your ears to the
utmost. Your skeleton grow heavy.

MRS BROADBENT: Could I have your full attention just for one
moment? Did anyone here do this? Speak up. No? Right.
As you were. Carry on.

(*She goes briskly out, leaving utter confusion in the Yoga class.*)

WOMAN: Bugger it. I was just going under.

12. INT. HOPKINS'S CLASSROOM. EVENING

HOPKINS *is lecturing.*

HOPKINS: . . . and a good deal has been written and continues
to be written about this small circle of friends around
Virginia Woolf, the circle we call the . . .

(MAUREEN *has her hand up.*)

Yes, Maureen?

MAUREEN: Bloomsbury Group.

(*General looks of distrust from the class.*)

HOPKINS: It wasn't a formal group. No membership cards. No
subscriptions. They didn't have meetings at set times. It
wasn't like this meeting here. We couldn't be the
Bloomsbury Group.

(MRS BROADBENT's *expression indicates "I don't see why
not."* MRS GARLAND *shakes her head implying "Of course
not."*)

Just a few like-minded people who kept running into one
another, dining together, gossiping. Common interests,
common assumptions, talking the same language, laughing
at the same jokes. But as a group ill-defined, vague and
amorphous.

(*He writes it up on the board.* SKINNER *has his hand up.*)

No, I know you know. Maureen, our dictionary lady.

(MAUREEN *looks up "amorphous" in a dictionary, which she
has backed in brown paper.*)

HOPKINS: (*Lecturing; voice under*) Virginia Woolf. Her husband
Leonard. Vanessa Bell, Virginia's sister. Clive Bell. The
painter Duncan Grant. Lytton Strachey. E. M. Forster.
These are what you might call hard-core Bloomsbury.

NARRATOR: (*Voice over*) Hopkins saw what vicars must feel like
Sunday after Sunday. The same people. The same sort of
people. Single ladies. Widows. Sad men. Refugees from
life. Except Skinner. Skinner had an ear-ring and one of
those thong things round his neck. Skinner was not a
refugee.

HOPKINS: Yes, Maureen?

MAUREEN: "Amorphous: shapeless, unorganized. Greek, *Morphos*. Form."

MR DODDS: I've got a better dictionary than that at home. It has wine lists.

MRS BROADBENT: Wine lists? In a dictionary?

MR DODDS: Vintage years. Plus the time in various parts of the world and the names of all the emergent countries.

HOPKINS: And at the centre of this circle, this coterie . . . (yes, if you want, Maureen) . . .

(MAUREEN *goes for the dictionary like a mad thing.*)

. . . Virginia Woolf herself. (*The now somewhat battered picture of Virginia Woolf.*) A sad lady. Nervous, highly strung . . .

MRS TUCKER: (*To* MISS GIBBONS) Like you.

HOPKINS: . . . who must always be asking "What is it like to be me here now?"

(SKINNER *puts his head down on his desk.*)

But it is ironical that a writer who struggled to pin down the moment in words and make it free of time and circumstances should be remembered chiefly as part of that time and these circumstances, the centre of that circle of friends . . . that coterie . . . yes, Maureen?

MAUREEN: "Set of persons associated by exclusive interests."

HOPKINS: So what I'd like to do if I could is to try and steer us back from her life to her work.

(MRS GARLAND *nods sagely.*)

(*Voice over*) Don't nod, sweetheart, you've never read a word. (*Aloud*) It has been said that the novel widens experience and poetry depends on it.

SKINNER: Who by?

HOPKINS: In this sense Mrs Woolf's work is nearer poetry . . . I think it was Harold Nicolson.

SKINNER: Christ.

HOPKINS: Why?

SKINNER: Nothing. I pass.

MRS GARLAND: Excuse me.

HOPKINS: (*Voice over*) Oh hell.

MRS GARLAND: . . . but didn't Harold Nicolson's wife Vita Sackville-West have a very intimate relationship with Virginia?

HOPKINS: (*Voice over*) Virginia! Mrs Woolf to you, you art-struck cow. (*Aloud*) Yes, she did.

MRS GARLAND: A relationship that was in part at least physical.

HOPKINS: That's open to debate.

SKINNER: Let's debate it then.

HOPKINS: Would there be any point? I don't think any of us have precise information. (*Voice over*) Or were you crouching in your Leavisite underpants in the wardrobe at the time? (*Aloud*) But while the facts of her life are not irrelevant to her work, I think I ought to . . . yes, Maureen?

MAUREEN: (*Who has her hand up*) Litotes. "Not irrelevant."

HOPKINS: Yes, Maureen. I think we ought to try and get back to the permanent record of her books.

MR DODDS: There's no tale to them, is there? That's where she leaves me. I like a good tale. Kipling, you see, he's different.

MRS TUCKER: Here we go again. He always tries and gets it on to Kipling.

MR DODDS: Well, I know about Kipling.

MRS BROADBENT: So do we now. We had him all last week.

MRS TUCKER: Whenever anybody suffers from nerves, which is what she suffered from, I say, "What's the hubby like?"

MISS GIBBONS: Yes. They're generally at the bottom of it.

MRS TUCKER: You see, she never had any children. If you've not had children you don't know what life's all about.

MISS GIBBONS: Yes. Except I haven't had children.

MAUREEN: Nor have I.

MRS GARLAND: She did have children. Her novels were her children.

MR DODDS: Then she's better off than me. I wish I'd had novels not daughters.

SKINNER: Why?

MR DODDS: Because novels don't have 15-year-old boyfriends. Novels don't come in with teeth marks on their neck. Novels don't hang around the bus station half the night waiting for the coach to come in from Catterick. Novels don't get pregnant.

MRS TUCKER: How is she?

MR DODDS: I don't want to talk about it.

Later in the lecture.

HOPKINS: In general her books are very decorous. They're concerned with feelings, impressions rather than actions. In the novels of Virginia Woolf we do not expect to come across a scantily clad blonde standing over a body with a smoking gun in her hand. Any more than in the novels of E. M. Forster do we follow a trail of discarded undies towards the bedroom. Undies do not lead to bedrooms or marriage to mayhem. But supposing they did would this be any more Life than a middle-aged lady sitting reading in a garden? (*Voice over*) Yes. Yes. It would. (*Aloud*) So if in the novels of Virginia Woolf and E. M. Forster there is not enough of what we call euphemistically life . . . (MAUREEN *reaches for the dictionary.*) No, Maureen. Are you looking up "euphemistically"? Don't. Look up "life".

MRS BROADBENT: Life? We all know what that means.

HOPKINS: She didn't. That was what she was always asking. What is life like?

SKINNER: Listen. If Virginia Woolf had been born in Brighouse she'd never have got off the ground.

MRS GARLAND: Is Brighouse the yardstick, I ask myself.

SKINNER: It is for me.

MRS BROADBENT: Well, some of us have wider horizons. We were in London only last week. And I have a son in Sutton Coldfield. Environment? Given a car and a good train service one transcends it.

SKINNER: Yeah. What need of art?

MR DODDS: A lot of these authors . . . and her in particular . . . I get the feeling they would have despised me. I mean, I'm doing them a favour, I think, reading their books. I know jolly well she'd have really looked down her snitch at me. Whereas it's funny I never get that feeling with Kipling.

HOPKINS: I think that's true. We go to literature for different reasons. Entertainment. Enlightenment. For inspiration. Consolation. A book can be a window on the world. It can also be a lens, to focus or magnify. But there is a sense too, as you say, in which the process works in reverse. Books are a window on ourselves. A lens under which we, not the world, are examined. Can we live up to them? Are we worthy of them? We feel got at by books. Disturbed. Our lives are called into question. In that sense we not only read books. Books read us. Yes, Maureen?

MAUREEN: (*Reading in her flat frightened voice*) "One. Life. State of functional activity and continual change peculiar to organized matter. Being alive. Two. Energy, liveliness, vivacity, animation. Three. Period from birth to death. Phrases as: True to . . . As large as . . . Get the fright of one's . . . The . . . and soul of the party. This is the . . . What a . . . Not on your . . . The time of one's . . ."

HOPKINS: Never mind.

MAUREEN: It goes on.

SKINNER: You bet.

HOPKINS: Forget it.

13. INT. HOPKINS'S CLASSROOM. EVENING
The lecture is over. HOPKINS *is just clearing up.* SKINNER *continues to sit there, although everyone else has gone. This*

makes HOPKINS *uneasy.*

HOPKINS: Do you want anything?

SKINNER: If I was to ask you out for a drink, would you come?

HOPKINS: Yes.

SKINNER: What? Like tonight?

HOPKINS: No, I can't. I mean, I'd have liked to, but . . .

SKINNER: Skip it.

(SKINNER *gets up and gets ready to go. He looks at the mutilated poster of Virginia Woolf.*)

I came across a story about her once. Your friend. She was caught short on a train and it didn't have a corridor. So she made this elaborate funnel out of *The Times* and did it out of the window.

(*He indicates how.*)

HOPKINS: I don't know why you come. You run rings round this lot. You know all the answers. Are you married?

(SKINNER *says nothing.*)

I don't mean to imply . . . that you're . . . oh Christ.

SKINNER: What?

HOPKINS: Nothing.

SKINNER: You don't mean what?

HOPKINS: Nothing. Never mind.

SKINNER: That's right. Never mind. Relax. I am married. Got one kid. And it's either this or watching colour TV. I think I prefer this.

HOPKINS: Do you?

SKINNER: Yes.

(SKINNER *has begun to clear up. He picks up the battered pictures.*)

HOPKINS: Tear that up.

SKINNER: You reckon?

HOPKINS: Yes.

SKINNER: It's council property. Well, love. Was it worth it? Look at the figures. Ten novels, five nervous breakdowns, no kids, one suicide. And this is where it's landed you,

sweetheart: a further education class in the Mechanics'
Institute, Halifax, on a wet Tuesday night in 1978. Let me
introduce you, Virginia, old love. Here it is. Posterity.
(*Puts her in the waste-paper basket.*) You're sure you don't
fancy that pint?

HOPKINS: Oh yes. I do.

SKINNER: Ditch her.

HOPKINS: I can't.

SKINNER: Let's all go. Have a threesome.

HOPKINS: No, that wouldn't be a good idea.
(*The* CARETAKER *comes in and starts straightening up the room
and grumbling.*)
Maybe we could go next week?

SKINNER: Sure. If you fancy. Next week. Week after. I don't
have a tight schedule.

CARETAKER: Comparative Literature. Comparative pigsty.
Look at all this. I don't know. You'd think it'd be Yoga
what would turn the place upside down. You go in the
Fortescue Room and it's a palace compared to this. What
do you do?

SKINNER: What do we do, Mr Hopkins? Well, we tend to kick
off with some fairly generalized sex-play, after which one of
the pensioners in the class is chased round the room and
violated by the rest. We then get down to some serious
E. M. Forster. What do you think we do?

CARETAKER: Don't you speak to me like that.

HOPKINS: Sorry.

SKINNER: No. Not sorry. With you it's too much sorry. Not
sorry at all. Look. This is a lecturer in Comparative
Literature. His job is throwing ideas about. You are a
caretaker. Your job is straightening up the chairs
afterwards. That's his work, this is your work. So stop
chuntering because if we each one of us does our work and
rejoices in it we shall all achieve salvation. Correct?
(*The* CARETAKER *is left open-mouthed.*)

HOPKINS: Sorry.
    (HOPKINS *and* SKINNER *go*.)

14. INT. CORRIDOR OUTSIDE HOPKINS'S CLASSROOM.
EVENING
SKINNER: I can't tempt you then?
    (WENDY *is coming along the corridor*.)
HOPKINS: Too late.
    (*As he passes her* SKINNER *winks*.)
SKINNER: Tonight's the night.
    (WENDY *takes* HOPKINS'*s arm*.)
WENDY: I don't like him. Don't you like me having my arm
    through yours?
HOPKINS: Yes, only . . .
WENDY: What?
HOPKINS: I'm busting.
WENDY: Well, go then.
HOPKINS: I can't here. It's a madhouse.

15. INT. GENTLEMEN'S LAVATORY. EVENING
HOPKINS *stands against an abstract background of tiles.*
NARRATOR: (*Voice over*) Hopkins ought to have ditched Wendy
    and gone with Skinner, instead of doing the right thing.
    He did not know it but he now loved Skinner. Doing the
    right thing is not always the right thing to do. Still, at
    least the lavatory was empty. Hopkins was one of those
    people who finds solitude in this department a *sine qua
    non.*
    (HOPKINS *moves over and stands in a stall. The door of the
    lavatory opens and a well-to-do middle-aged* MAN *comes in.
    He stands next to* HOPKINS.)
    (*Voice over*) Too late. With anybody there he could not go.
    While his neighbour discharged in a confident Niagara . . .
    (*We hear the sound of an assured piss.*)
    . . . all Hopkins could do was wait. In one stall the mighty

Zambezi; in the other the Aswan Dam. And so
Hopkins waited.
(*The* MAN *finishes pissing and washes his hands. He dries his
hands with* HOPKINS *still waiting in the stall unable to
discharge. The* MAN *comes up behind* HOPKINS *and speaks
into his ear.*)

MAN: This toilet is only a stone's throw from the West
Yorkshire Constabulary. You're playing with fire.
(*The* MAN *goes.* HOPKINS *heaves a sigh of relief and we hear
him begin to piss.*)

PART THREE

16. INT. WENDY'S FLAT. NIGHT

HOPKINS *and* WENDY *are sitting in silence.*

WENDY: Trevor. Am I boring you?

HOPKINS: No. No. Why.

WENDY: I just thought you seemed a bit bored, that's all. Are you?

HOPKINS: No. I'm not bored. Are you bored?

WENDY: Me? No.

HOPKINS: That's good.

    (*Long pause.*)

WENDY: Trevor.

HOPKINS: What?

WENDY: It's good when you feel you don't have to talk.

HOPKINS: When?

WENDY: When you feel you understand one another so well you don't need to say anything.

HOPKINS: Say what?

WENDY: Anything.

HOPKINS: Why, what do you want to say?

WENDY: Nothing. (*Pause.*) My parents had that.

HOPKINS: What?

WENDY: This unspoken understanding. They could sit with each other in utter silence and each know what the other was thinking. (*Pause.*) So there was no point in saying it. Of course they spoke sometimes. I'm not saying that. Factual information.

HOPKINS: Yes. I suppose if the cistern was overflowing somebody would have to speak. Or the cat had been sick in the piano.

WENDY: You stamp on poetry, Trevor.

Later.

WENDY: Trevor.

HOPKINS: What?

WENDY: I think when one is married . . .

NARRATOR: (*Voice over*) She meant "we".

WENDY: And I don't mean "we", I think when one is married it is terrifically important that one's children should see one naked. Don't you think so?

NARRATOR: No.

HOPKINS: Up to a point.

WENDY: One of the saddest things in my childhood was that I never saw my father naked. And now it's too late.

HOPKINS: He's not dead.

WENDY: No, but he's got a plastic hip. One ought to be able to see that the body has its own special beauty at every age. Not merely the bodies of the young. The middle-aged body, that has a beauty. The aged body. One of the most beautiful people I've ever seen was . . . you won't believe this . . . Gandhi.

HOPKINS: Yes. He wasn't exactly sexy though, was he?

WENDY: Have you ever seen your mother bare?

HOPKINS: I don't want to think about it.

WENDY: Poor Trevor.

(*She goes into the kitchen.*)

HOPKINS: That flaming name again.

NARRATOR: (*Voice over*) Did he say he couldn't stay all night now or afterwards? Afterwards.

HOPKINS: I can't stay all night.

(WENDY *comes back.*)

WENDY: What did you say?

HOPKINS: Nothing.

WENDY: Why?

HOPKINS: I have to teach first thing.

WENDY: So have I.

HOPKINS: I've got my laundry to get ready.

WENDY: Why don't you say, "To hell with my laundry"? Live, Trevor.

HOPKINS: Live! This!

WENDY: What I'd like is if we were both to take our clothes off and just sit. Not do anything. Just be. I like your way of being, Trevor. I think one is a different person with one's clothes off. A more natural person. More real. I am anyway. You are too.

HOPKINS: Yes.

NARRATOR: (*Voice over*) On the contrary. This was the real him. The one in the shirt, pullover and nasty Terylene trousers. Get all that off and he didn't know who he was.

WENDY: As I see it the body is the basic syntax in the grammar of humanism.

NARRATOR: (*Voice over*) Why did they have to wade through this every time? Other people got foreplay. All he got was *The Joys of Yoga*.

WENDY: Where are you going?

HOPKINS: The lav.

17. INT. WENDY'S BEDROOM. NIGHT

WENDY *is in bed. The bedside light is on.* HOPKINS *begins to undress and, as he does so, turns off the light. As he is getting his shirt over his head* WENDY *leans over and switches it on again. He leaves the light on for a moment or two but just before taking off his trousers switches it off again. And so on. And off. And on. But when* HOPKINS *finally makes it into bed the light is off.*

WENDY: Why can't we have the light on? I can't see my hand in front of my face.

HOPKINS: It's not in front of your face, is it?

WENDY: I want to see you, Trevor.

HOPKINS: I don't want to see myself.

WENDY: I want you to see me.

HOPKINS: What for?

WENDY: Trevor. I want to see you seeing me.

HOPKINS: Well, I wouldn't anyway, would I, light or no light.
I've not got my glasses on.

WENDY: Trevor.

(*Pause*.)

HOPKINS: Wendy.

WENDY: What, Trevor?

HOPKINS: Do you mind not saying my name so much.

WENDY: Why, Trevor?

HOPKINS: There, that. Trevor. Like that. Try not to say it so
much.

WENDY: Why, darling?

(*Pause*.)

HOPKINS: Not really "darling", either.

WENDY: What am I to call you?

HOPKINS: You. That's fine. Call me you.

WENDY: Oh Trevor.

NARRATOR: (*Voice over*) A yoga instructress and supple as an
eel. She would do anything. Some people would give their
right arm to be here.

WENDY: What's the matter?

HOPKINS: You're lying on my right arm.

WENDY: Sorry.

NARRATOR: (*Voice over*) What Hopkins wanted . . . it was only
part of his problem . . . but what he wanted was someone
who didn't want him. He had such a low opinion of himself
that if someone wanted him that must mean they weren't
worth having.

HOPKINS: Why?

WENDY: Why what?

HOPKINS: Nothing. I was just being cosmic.

WENDY: Oh Trevor. Trevor?

HOPKINS: What?

WENDY: I couldn't put on some Bruckner, could I?

HOPKINS: Yes. Anything.

WENDY: I'll slip my kimono on. I want to stay warm for you,

Trevor.
(WENDY *goes to the record player.*)
NARRATOR: (*Voice over*) Hopkins wondered if Hemingway had
   ever had to go through this rigmarole. Or Kafka. Or
   Leonard Woolf, the poor, frustrated sod. Oh shut it,
   Virginia. This is the only lighthouse you're going to.
WENDY: What are you thinking about?
HOPKINS: Virginia Woolf.
WENDY: You're a true scholar, Trevor. I can't find Bruckner.
   You've no objection to Mahler?
   (*She puts on* Das Lied von der Erde. *Fade out on her
   advancing towards the bed.*)

Afterwards. WENDY *is in bed.* HOPKINS *is dressing by the light of
the gas fire.*
HOPKINS: Night, night.
   (*But she is asleep. He turns the gas fire off.*)

18. EXT. DESERTED STREET. NIGHT
HOPKINS *is waiting at a bus stop.*
HOPKINS: That's it. Temporary membership of the human race.
   For half an hour, maybe, I join. Get a green card. Am like
   everybody else. We have seen the Lions of Longleat. O my
   pale life.
   (*A bus comes. He gets on.*)

19. INT. BUS. NIGHT
HOPKINS *sits downstairs, just inside the door on the seat nearest the*
CONDUCTOR. *There is nobody opposite. Book on his lap. The West
Indian* CONDUCTOR *takes the fare. The bus stops. A* BOY *and*
GIRL *get on. Sit opposite him. The* BOY *with his arm round the*
GIRL.
   The BOY *and* GIRL *begin to kiss passionately.* HOPKINS *opens his
book. Deep devouring unashamed passion. He looks up from his
book and catches the* GIRL's *open eyes looking over the* BOY's

69

shoulder as he kisses her neck. Looks away. He looks at his book.
The GIRL *whispers to the* BOY *while kissing his ear. The* BOY *looks*
across at him. He kisses her again. Looking while he kisses.
HOPKINS *does not look up. He reads. The bus is stopping. The* BOY
and GIRL *lurch to their feet.*

BOY: You want to watch it, you.

HOPKINS: Me?

BOY: Just watch it.

GIRL: Yeah.

BOY: You want to watch what you're watching. Creep.

> (*The* BOY *hits him hard in the face. The bus stops. They get off.*
> HOPKINS's *book has dropped on the floor. The* CONDUCTOR,
> *impassive throughout, picks up the book.*)

CONDUCTOR: Your nose be real bleeding, man.

> (HOPKINS *feels his nose.*)
>
> De bus gone go past the Infirmary. Gone drop you in the
> Infirmary, man?
>
> (HOPKINS *nods. The* CONDUCTOR *rings a ticket.*) 'nother 5p.

20. EXT. STREET. NIGHT

The bus stops and HOPKINS *gets off. Waiting at the bus stop to get*
on is SKINNER.

SKINNER: Hello. What's been happening to you, then?

> (SKINNER *turns back with* HOPKINS *and they walk towards*
> *the Infirmary.*)

21. INT. THE INFIRMARY. NIGHT

HOPKINS *and* SKINNER *are sitting in the out-patients clinic. A*
WOMAN *sits beside* HOPKINS *and opposite* ANOTHER WOMAN
weeps helplessly.

SKINNER: Do you fancy a coffee?

HOPKINS: Yes. Do you?

SKINNER: Do you take sugar?

HOPKINS: No.

> (SKINNER *goes off for some coffee. The* WOMAN OPPOSITE

continues to weep and in order not to look at her HOPKINS, *his nose bleeding still, opens his book. He reads for a while or tries to, but an out-patients' in Halifax is not the best place to read Virginia Woolf, particularly with a bloody nose. The* WOMAN *beside him looks at him curiously.*)

WOMAN: Love. Love. Your blood's going all over your book. Blood, love. It's all over your book.

(HOPKINS *closes his book.*)

NARRATOR: (*Voice over*) Hopkins felt sick. He had a headache and his nose hurt. The woman crying embarrassed him. The evening had not been a success. He put away his book.

(SKINNER *appears at the end of the corridor bringing coffee.*)

(*Voice over*) It would be months before he opened it again, but when he did and saw the blood blotted on the pages he found he looked back to that night as a happy one. Without believing in corners that night he had turned one.

SKINNER: What's up with her do you think?

HOPKINS: I don't know.

NARRATOR: (*Voice over*) Something had happened.

SKINNER: "Never mind." (*Raises his cup and smiles.*) Cheers . . . Trev. (HOPKINS *smiles too.*)

HOPKINS: Cheers . . . Dave.

(*We freeze frame on the bloody but smiling face of* HOPKINS *as the music from* South Pacific *swells. In the final credits sequence,* HOPKINS *shares the frozen frame with* SKINNER, *who is also smiling. But it is* HOPKINS *whose smile is wicked.* SKINNER *looks rather fond. The words of the song make it plain that this has been a love story.*)

I'm not ashamed to reveal
The world-famous feeling I feel.

I'm as corny as Kansas in August,
I'm as normal as blueberry pie,
No more a smart little girl with no heart,

I have found me a wonderful guy!

I am in a conventional dither
With a conventional star in my eye.
And you will note there's a lump in my throat
When I speak of that wonderful guy!

I'm as trite and as gay as a daisy in May,
A cliché coming true!
I'm bromidic and bright as a moon-happy night,
Pouring light on the dew!

I'm as corny as Kansas in August,
High as a flag on the Fourth of July!
If you'll excuse an expression I use,
I'm in love, I'm in love, I'm in love, I'm in love,
I'm in love with a wonderful guy!

ALL DAY ON THE SANDS

CHARACTERS

COLIN COOPER
DAD (MR COOPER)
MAM (MRS COOPER)
KEITH
JO
MRS CATTLEY
FAY
MR CATTLEY
MRS THORNTON
MR THORNTON
JENNIFER COOPER
HARRY
ALBERT
MAN IN THE ICE-CREAM PARLOUR
WOMAN IN THE ICE-CREAM PARLOUR
MAN AT THE BOATING POOL
GRAHAM
DEREK'S FATHER
DEREK
DEREK'S MOTHER
HILDA
LESLIE

HOLIDAY-MAKERS, SHOP ASSISTANTS, etc.

All Day on the Sands was first transmitted by London Weekend Television on 24 February 1979. The cast included:

COLIN COOPER	Gary Carp
DAD	Alun Armstrong
MAM	Marjorie Yates
KEITH	Jonathan Coy
JO	Rosalind Wilson
MRS CATTLEY	Jane Freeman
FAY	Helene Palmer
MR CATTLEY	Ken Jones
MRS THORNTON	Lynne Carol
MR THORNTON	Clifford Kershaw
JENNIFER COOPER	Susan Hopkins
HARRY	Harry Markham
ALBERT	Albert Modley
MAN AT THE BOATING POOL	Bernard Atha
GRAHAM	Stephen Greenwood
DEREK'S FATHER	Bert Gaunt
DEREK	Lee Atkins
DEREK'S MOTHER	Liz Dawn
HILDA	Paula Tilbrook
LESLIE	Denis Bond
Producer	Stephen Frears
Director	Giles Foster
Designer	James Weatherup
Music	George Fenton

PART ONE

1. EXT. TOWN. DAY
A view across roofs, through chimneypots, television aerials and the backs of boarding houses towards the distant glitter of the sea. It is early morning.

2. INT. BOARDING HOUSE: TOP-FLOOR CORRIDOR. DAY
COLIN, *a boy of 12 closes a bedroom door. He walks along corridors, up and down two or three steps, round corners. A house that has been extended and converted. Through various fire doors until he comes to another corridor and knocks on a door.*
COLIN: (*A bit nervously*) Mam . . . Mam. Mam?
   (DAD *opens the door. A man in his late thirties. In pyjamas.*)
DAD: What? What's the matter?
COLIN: What time is it?

3. INT. BOARDING HOUSE: COOPERS' BEDROOM. DAY
COLIN *gets past his* FATHER *into the room, which is dark. His* MOTHER *is asleep.*
DAD: What time do you think it is, coming in first thing? It's not seven o'clock yet.
COLIN: Mam.
DAD: You don't wake your Mam. Your Mam's on holiday.
COLIN: Mam.
   (DAD *gets hold of* COLIN *and pushes him out of the room.*)
MAM: What is it? Colin?
DAD: What do you want to be getting us up at this time for?
COLIN: I've nothing to do.
DAD: Well, we haven't anything for you to do.
MAM: Read, love.
DAD: Out.

77

4. INT. BOARDING HOUSE: TOP-FLOOR CORRIDOR. DAY
COLIN *goes back down the corridor. As he is going the bedroom door opens again and* DAD *puts his head out.*
DAD: And Colin. Don't wake our Jennifer.

5. INT. BOARDING HOUSE: COOPERS' BEDROOM. DAY
DAD *gets back into bed.*
MAM: (*Turning over and going back to sleep*) What did he want?
DAD: Shooting. Quarter to seven. (*Pause.*) Turn to me.
MAM: No.

6. INT. BOARDING HOUSE: TOP-FLOOR CORRIDOR. DAY
COLIN *goes back to his bedroom. More slowly. Fiddling with things. Spitting carefully into a fire bucket. Looking out of odd windows. Very quiet.*

7. INT. BOARDING HOUSE: COLIN'S AND JENNIFER'S BEDROOM. DAY
Colin's unmade bed. A little GIRL *asleep in another bed. She is between 9 and 12. He wanders about the room. Looks at her. Maybe plays with her teddy. He sits in front of the three-panel dressing-table mirror and adjusts it carefully so that he can see a view of the back of his head.*

  He opens the window and looks out at the back of the boarding house. A version of the shot we saw at the start. A medley of roofs and extensions. Below Colin's window a flat roof, about two storeys down.

  There are a few pebbles in the room, obviously ones the little girl has collected. He takes them and drops them one by one on to the roof below, trying to hit an empty bottle which is standing there.

  He finishes all the pebbles. He looks round the room. He picks up his sister's sandal and looks round for some string.

8. INT. BOARDING HOUSE: JO'S AND KEITH'S BEDROOM. DAY
A bedroom on the floor below. JO *and* KEITH, *a young couple on*

their honeymoon, are in bed. KEITH *is lying on his back.* JO *half on top of him.*

KEITH: Jo.

JO: What?

KEITH: There's something banging on the window.

JO: Who cares.

    (*Pause.*)

KEITH: Where's my pyjama bottoms?

JO: I don't know. You took them off.

KEITH: *You* took them off. Where are they?

9. INT. BOARDING HOUSE: COLIN'S AND JENNIFER'S BEDROOM. DAY

Cut to COLIN *upstairs dangling the sandal on a string out of the window.*

10. INT. BOARDING HOUSE: JO'S AND KEITH'S BEDROOM. DAY

KEITH *is looking out of the window.*

KEITH: Jo.

JO: What?

KEITH: It's a sandal.

JO: Come on back to bed.

KEITH: It's a sandal on a string.

JO: We've not been married five minutes and all you're interested in is sandals on strings.

KEITH: Well, life has to go on. He's trying to knock over that bottle. He's trying to knock that bottle over, Jo. Missed it that time. He's having another go. Now he's in trouble.

JO: If I'd wanted a running commentary I'd have married Eddie Waring. Come back to bed.

KEITH: He's lost his sandal. His sandal's come off.

    (*We see the empty string going up past the window.*)

JO: (*As* KEITH *comes back to bed*) Flaming sandal. Come here.

11. INT. BOARDING HOUSE. COLIN'S AND JENNIFER'S BEDROOM. DAY
Cut to COLIN *in the bedroom upstairs, pulling in the string and looking down at the sandal on the flat roof.*

12. INT. BOARDING HOUSE: KITCHEN. DAY
MRS CATTLEY, *the landlady, is cooking breakfast. She is busy putting out delicate scalloped pieces of butter on to tiny plates. Two to a plate. She puts three on one plate and with her fingers edges the extra one on to another plate.*

MRS CATTLEY: Two pats per person. Butter's bad for you anyway. It's been proved in America. I'm doing them a favour.
(FAY, *an oldish waitress, is scraping toast.*)

FAY: Marmalade. Where's the bloody marmalade?
(MRS CATTLEY *holds a sauce bottle up to the light.*)

MRS CATTLEY: Look at the level of that sauce! Only started yesterday and it's gone down dramatically. I'm under no compulsion to provide sauce. Lathering it on. It's not as if my cooking needed sauce.

FAY: You want to make it available on request. "Sauce available on request." That might bring them to a sense of responsibility.

MRS CATTLEY: I wouldn't care but they go at the salt and pepper like mad things. You'd think they'd never seen a cruet in their lives. Pigs. Pigs' tea. Pigs' toast. Pigs' marmalade.
(*Two tones on the Tannoy herald an announcement and a look of long-suffering contempt comes over* MRS CATTLEY's *face as we hear her husband begin his announcement.*)

MR CATTLEY: (*Over Tannoy*) Hi, all you leisure lovers. Eight o'clock, the temperature is 52 degrees and it's fair to cloudy in mid-town Morecambe. This is your Miramar host, Percy Cattley, saying hello again and welcome to another fun-packed day.

13. INT. BOARDING HOUSE: HALL. DAY
Cut to the hall where MR CATTLEY *has a little cubbyhole under the stairs from which he broadcasts.*

MR CATTLEY: (*Continuing*) The service of breakfast will shortly be commencing in the Portofino Room. Top of this morning's menu are kippers, fresh in from Fleetwood, the best Poulton le Fylde can do in the way of bacon plus free-range eggs and your choice of starters: orange juice, pineapple juice, tomato juice, grapefruit segments, or melon balls.
(*In the doorway we see* COLIN *looking up inside the shaft of the dumb-waiter.*)
Leave that alone, unless you want decapitating.
(COLIN *watches him expressionlessly, which makes* MR CATTLEY *slightly self-conscious.*)
May I remind you that breakfast is from eight until nine thirty so Mrs Cattley and I look forward to seeing you shortly in the Portofino Room.

MRS CATTLEY: (*Coming through with some dishes*) And no latecomers.

MR CATTLEY: So rush, rush, rush to the Portofino Room.
(*The two tones go, indicating the end of transmission.*)

14. INT. BOARDING HOUSE: PORTOFINO ROOM. DAY
Empty. Not all the tables are set. The place is plainly not full.
COLIN *sits at a table for four.* FAY *ignores him.*

FAY: I'm not serving you, young man. There's four of you. You'd better wait till you've got a full complement. Yes?
(*She waits to take the order of an older couple who have come in and sat down at the next table. Conscious of her presence, the couple communicate in an undertone.*)

MRS THORNTON: I thought I might try the kippers this morning but I don't know whether I dare. They have a tendency to repeat. What do you think?

MR THORNTON: If you want them, have them.

MRS THORNTON: I don't know whether I do.

MR THORNTON: Well, have bacon.

MRS THORNTON: Shall I?

MR THORNTON: She's waiting.

MRS THORNTON: What are *you* having?

MR THORNTON: Bacon. She'll have bacon. And I'll have bacon too. (FAY *goes away*.)

MRS THORNTON: I wanted kippers.

FAY: (*Out of vision, as* COLIN *gets up and goes out*) Two bacon.

15. INT. BOARDING HOUSE: UPSTAIRS CORRIDOR. DAY
The corridor leading to Colin's and Jennifer's room. Piped music.
MAM *walking with* JENNIFER, *one shoe on, one off.*

MAM: Do you remember taking it off?

JENNIFER: Yes.

MAM: Well, it must be there somewhere.

16. INT. BOARDING HOUSE: COLIN'S AND JENNIFER'S
BEDROOM. DAY
MAM *looks under the bed. In the empty echoing drawers of the dressing table. In the vast wardrobe.*

MAM: You'd better put your best on.

JENNIFER: They hurt.

MAM: That's your look-out.

JENNIFER: My feet get hot.

MAM: I'll clatter you if you're not careful. Where is it?
(*She looks in the bottom of the wardrobe. Through the open door we hear the sound of the Tannoy . . .*)

MR CATTLEY: (*Over the Tannoy*) . . . the finest Fleetwood kippers, plus free-range eggs and your choice of starters: orange juice, grapefruit juice, tomato juice, grapefruit segments or melon balls. Service of breakfast in the Portofino Room will be terminating in approximately ten minutes' time and I am asked to say that staff shortages and the prevailing economic climate make it impossible to serve latecomers.

MAM: Where do you think we find money for new sandals now
    we've naught coming in? It doesn't run to new sandals,
    Social Security.

17. INT. BOARDING HOUSE: STAIRS/LANDING. DAY
DAD *waiting at the head of the stairs.*
DAD: Lil! Lil!
MAM: (*Out of vision*) Coming.

18. INT. BOARDING HOUSE: STAIRS/HALL. DAY
MAM, DAD, COLIN *and* JENNIFER *are going downstairs.*
MAM: And think on, don't let on.
JENNIFER: What?
MAM: You know. About your Dad. And Colin, you neither.

19. INT. BOARDING HOUSE: PORTOFINO ROOM. DAY
One or two more GUESTS *have appeared. The* THORNTONS *are still
there at the next table to* MAM *and* DAD, *(whose name is Cooper). A
youngish* MAN *and somewhat older* WOMAN *are at another table.
The* COOPERS *have sat down when* KEITH *and* JO, *the honeymoon
couple, get in at the last minute, nearly knocking down* MRS
CATTLEY *who is coming out as they are going in.*

20. INT. BOARDING HOUSE: KITCHEN. DAY
MRS CATTLEY: It always has to be the last minute. I could be
    serving breakfast while twelve o'clock and they'd still be
    poling in at two minutes to.
MR CATTLEY: They're honeymooners, Denise. I like to think
    that at the Miramar we give them a bit of elbow room.
MRS CATTLEY: Oh, is that what it's called – elbow room? Sex
    till a hair's breadth of nine thirty and it's elbow room.
    Well listen, Alvar Liddell, I'm the one that wants elbow
    room.

21. INT. BOARDING HOUSE: PORTOFINO ROOM. DAY

FAY *is taking the* COOPERS' *order.*

FAY: Segments. Segments. Segments. I've got three segments.

COLIN: (*Whispering to his* MAM) I can't have flakes and segments?

MAM: No. He can't have flakes and segments?

FAY: No. That's your choice of starters.

COLIN: (*Whispering to his* MAM) What if I didn't have scrambled egg?

MAM: What if he didn't have scrambled egg?

FAY: I can't be doing permutations on it. Flakes or segments?

COLIN: Flakes.

MAM: (*Whispering*) Jennifer'll give you some of her flakes.

JENNIFER: I won't.

MAM: You've lost your sandal, miss. You'll do as you're told.

JENNIFER: Dad.

DAD: Do as you're told.

MAM: You two, you do show us up.

MR THORNTON: Grand day again.

DAD: Ay.

MR THORNTON: Mind you, May, it generally is nice. They've proved that statistically. Jodrell Bank.

MRS THORNTON: But it's funny, I was saying to Edgar, we always seem to hit on a good week weatherwise. We did last year, didn't we, Edgar? Never saw a drop of rain.

MR THORNTON: We always try and get in before the crowds. There's not much going off but we like that.

MRS THORNTON: We like that. July, it gets a bit common. You get all sorts nowadays.

MAM: Oh, yes. Jennifer, sit still. And put your feet under the table. She's lost her shoe.

MR THORNTON: Cinderella.

MAM: Last year we went to Minorca, only we thought we'd have a change this year.

MRS THORNTON: Oh. Majorca.

MAM: Minorca. It's the adjacent island.

MR THORNTON: Frankly, I wouldn't thank you for Majorca. Minorca. Any of those places. I always say to Hetty when we go out on a morning, "Breathe in, Hetty. You'll not find finer air in the whole of the Western Hemisphere."

MRS THORNTON: And he knows. He was in Malaya during the Emergency.

(MAM *is watching the older woman,* HILDA, *and the younger man,* LESLIE. *They look happy.*)

This is his special marmalade. No (*mouthing*) sugar.

MAM: Jack could do with slimming. I'm always on to Jack to slim.

MRS THORNTON: No. He's (*mouthing*) diabetic. He can be going along right as rain. The next minute he's in a coma. I watch him like a hawk. Whereas ten years ago he would have been a dead man, he now has his special marmalade and he's champion. It's what I say, you learn to accommodate.

MAM: You have to.

MRS THORNTON: It's like my sister-in-law. She's only got half a stomach yet she leads a perfectly normal life.

MAM: Where's that?

MRS THORNTON: Batley.

(MAM *watches the* HONEYMOONERS.)

MAM: Do you think they're married?

DAD: Which?

MAM: Them two.

DAD: I don't know. Ask them. Why?

MAM: They're only young if they are. Could we have a drop more hot water?

MR THORNTON: What's on the agenda for today?

MAM: I don't think we'll go far.

FAY: (*Out of vision, shouting down the hatch*) More hot water now.

MR THORNTON: We had quite a hectic day at Heysham yesterday so we're not going to overdo it. Hetty wants to see if she can pick out a frock and I've some business to transact at the Post Office. We'll probably stagger down to the beach later on.

MAM: I don't think we'll get much further than the sands today.

MR THORNTON: Well, that's what it's all about, isn't it? Giving yourself time to unwind. What's your line of thing?

(*There is a perceptible moment of awkwardness.*)

DAD: Well, I'm . . .

MAM: He works at this engineering firm in Leeds. Leeds. Engineering.

DAD: I'm a supervisor. Components.

MR THORNTON: Oh, *components*. They're the thing these days. I'm self-employed.

MRS THORNTON: We have a little gents outfitters. He goes in, but he's more or less semi-retired now, aren't you, Edgar?

MAM: One of these old family firms. He's been very happy there. They think the world of him.

MRS THORNTON: Well, they're the best, aren't they? There's that much redundancy now.

MR THORNTON: Well, Alice, there is and there isn't.

MRS THORNTON: Yes, I think there's work if you really scout around.

MAM: Oh yes, I'm sure there is.

MR THORNTON: A lot of these fellers, if they can get themselves as far as the labour exchange they reckon they've done a week's work.

DAD: That's right.

MRS THORNTON: Shocking.

(*The* CHILDREN *say nothing. At the* HONEYMOONERS' *table . . .*)

JO: What do you want to do today?

KEITH: I don't know. What do you want to do?

JO: I don't know. We'll do what you want to do.

KEITH: I want to do what you want to do.

JO: I don't want to do anything in particular. You know. I just want to be together.

KEITH: But we have to be together doing something. Would you like to go to Fleetwood?

22. INT. BOARDING HOUSE: HALL. DAY
The COOPERS *have come out of the Portofino Room.*
MRS CATTLEY *is waiting.*
MRS CATTLEY: Mrs Cooper. No bare feet in the Portofino Room, if you don't mind.
MAM: She's lost her shoe.
MRS CATTLEY: It's a rule of the house. We have to draw the line or else they'll be waltzing in in bikinis.
(*The* THORNTONS *have overheard this.*)
MAM: (*To* JENNIFER) You don't half show us up.
MR CATTLEY: (*Into Tannoy, voice under preceding dialogue*) Our dish of the day this evening will be duck à l'orange: fresh Aylesbury duckling in a tangy orange sauce together with crisp Norfolk peas and duchesse potatoes. There'll be another chance to sample Mrs Cattley's famous trifle, followed by After Eight mints and a choice of beverages.
MRS THORNTON: This regime suits us. We generally have our main meal at night.
MR CATTLEY: (*Into Tannoy*) Those patrons who have ordered lunchboxes will find them waiting for them now in the Marbella Lounge. Weight-watchers are recommended to try our slimline lunch pack specially selected to form part of your calorie-controlled diet. May I also remind patrons that Messrs Heaps run luxury coach trips every evening to specially selected beauty spots. Venue for this evening's trip is Newby Bridge, Mecca for the discerning sightseer. Patrons are advised to book early to avoid disappointment.

23. INT. BOARDING HOUSE: KITCHEN. DAY
MRS CATTLEY *is up to her elbows in greasy water, trying to unblock the sink.* FAY *is piling up the dirty plates. Over the Tannoy comes the end of* MR CATTLEY'*s morning transmission.*

MR CATTLEY: (*Voice over*) Patrons are particularly requested to
return their lunchboxes together with their plastic utensils.
There is a receptacle for returned utensils in the vestibule.
Have a good day now.

MRS CATTLEY: When Emperor Rosko comes off the air tell him
the sink's blocked.

24. INT. BOARDING HOUSE: MAM'S AND DAD'S BEDROOM. DAY

MAM: Has she come out? Jennifer. Go watch to see when she
comes out. You'd think they could run to more than one
toilet per floor, wouldn't you? It's with them being so hot on
fire regulations. They spend all the money on that and toilets
have to take a back seat. Have you looked for that shoe?

COLIN: I can't find it.

DAD: You'd better find it. I'm not budgeting for new shoes.

25. INT. BOARDING HOUSE: CORRIDOR. DAY

JENNIFER *is waiting smack outside the WC. Door opens. A* WOMAN
comes out.

(*Calling*) Mam! She's out.

26. INT. BOARDING HOUSE: MAM'S AND DAD'S BEDROOM. DAY

MAM: I'll wait a minute. I never like to see who's been in before
me.
(*She waits.*)

27. INT. BOARDING HOUSE: CORRIDOR. DAY

JENNIFER: Somebody else went in.

MAM: Well, go and look for your sandal, go on.

28. INT. BOARDING HOUSE: COLIN'S AND JENNIFER'S ROOM.
DAY

JENNIFER: You look.

COLIN: No.

JENNIFER: Why?

COLIN: What's the use?

JENNIFER: I don't like these shoes. I wish we were in Minorca. I never wore shoes.

29. INT. BOARDING HOUSE: PORTOFINO ROOM. DAY

FAY *is sitting at a table in the window in the now empty dining room having her breakfast. Through the window we see the* THORNTONS *going out, followed by the* COOPERS.

FAY: Glued to that flaming microphone. There's I don't know what swilling around in that sink and all he does is broadcast. Over and out. Well, I'm over and out after thirty-five breakfasts and nineteen early morning teas. What about my varicose veins? He wants to broadcast them. Pete sodding Murray. I'm jiggered . . .

(MR CATTLEY *passes and overhears her chuntering.*)

MR CATTLEY: Well, why do you do it then, Fay? We're not forcing you.

(*He goes upstairs.*)

FAY: Why? Because I'm saving up for some decent teeth. Some proper, private teeth. Some teeth that fit. I want teeth I can eat toast with. (*Tries to eat a slice of toast.*) Nay, I can't eat this toast.

30. EXT. STREET. DAY

The COOPERS *and the* THORNTONS *walking towards the promenade.*

MRS THORNTON: We like Morecambe. Blackpool's a bit on the common side. Morecambe's more refined. Only they're trying to spoil it here now. Discos. Miss World.

MAM: It's nice for the kiddies.

MRS THORNTON: Yes, only it's all kiddies now, isn't it?

MR THORNTON: (*Talking to* DAD) We debated whether or not to bring the car but parking's the problem. Everywhere's the same these days. It's not worth running a car. Are you motorized?

DAD: We've just got the mini but the suspension was a bit dodgy so I thought we wouldn't risk it.

MR THORNTON: I know the feeling. When you've got a couple of hours to spare I'll tell you the saga of my clutch.

DAD: Oh ay.

31. EXT. PROMENADE. DAY

MR *and* MRS THORNTON *and the* COOPERS *going along the promenade.*

MRS THORNTON: There's just that nice breeze.

MR THORNTON: We can't do with it too hot, can we, Hetty?

MRS THORNTON: No, Edgar can't do with it too hot and I can't either.

MR THORNTON: That's another reason why we steer clear of abroad. It does tend to be sweltering.

MRS THORNTON: Then there's the language problem. I have to think of him, you see. Say he went into a coma. I couldn't explain that in Spanish.

MR THORNTON: No, it's overrated is abroad.

MRS THORNTON: And he knows. He was in Malaya.

MR THORNTON: If I had to choose between Morecambe and Kuala Lumpur I'd plump for Morecambe any day. Just look at that!
(*Stops to survey the view across the bay.*) You wouldn't find that in Kuala Lumpur! Torremolinos neither.

32. EXT. BEACH. DAY

The COOPERS *have got two deckchairs and are walking along the sands.*

DAD: What's matter with here?

MAM: No.
(*She walks on.*)

DAD: Why? Why?

MAM: What do you think them seagulls are? That's a sewage pipe.

(*She indicates a spot five hundred yards out in the bay*.)

DAD: There?

MAM: It washes in. It has to go somewhere.

DAD: Well, be sharp or else we'll be in Grange. Here?

JENNIFER: Mam. I'm cold. I'm cold, Mam.

MAM: Well, all right, then.

DAD: Right. Your Mam's approved the site.

(*They set up deckchairs and* JENNIFER *begins to put her costume on*.)

What're you putting your costume on for if you're cold?

JENNIFER: It's the seaside.

MAM: Aren't you going to put your trunks on?

(COLIN *shakes his head*)

Nobody's looking.

COLIN: I don't want to, anyway.

33. EXT. BEACH. DAY

JENNIFER *has a child's book about seashore life*.

JENNIFER: There's none of these here. Dad.

DAD: What?

JENNIFER: There's none of these here.

(DAD *looks at her book*.)

DAD: There's shells. What more do you want?

JENNIFER: Starfish.

DAD: There aren't starfish at Morecambe. There aren't starfish anywhere much now.

JENNIFER: Crabs?

DAD: There'll be some crabs. Only they'll be fiddling little 'uns. You can't expect MacFisheries' crabs. Ask Colin to show you.

JENNIFER: He won't.

DAD: Play with your bucket and spade, then. Your Mam'll take you to look later on. (*Picks up the book*.) "Marine Life." Crabs. Lobsters. Look at that! Sea-horses. I've never seen a sea-horse in my life. And starfish. It's not fair. Putting ideas into their heads. It makes them disappointed. Even the shells. There's none of them shells, is there.

MAM: You can buy them in shops. Proper shells. You can't expect to find them just lying around.

34. EXT. BEACH. DAY

DAD: The tides are controlled by the moon. Did you know that?

COLIN: Yes.

DAD: How? You didn't.

COLIN: I did. We did it at school.

DAD: You didn't, did you?

MAM: Didn't what?

DAD: Know the moon controls the tides.

MAM: Well, it's not out.

DAD: What do you mean?

MAM: The moon. It's not out. So how can it control them?

DAD: It doesn't have to be out, does it, Colin? Your Mam thinks it has to be out first. It's up there somewhere, and it controls the tides.

MAM: Do you mean if it's a full moon the tide's up and if it's not it's only half-way?

(*Pause.*)

DAD: I think it's more complicated than that. Do you know, Colin?

COLIN: No.

DAD: I thought you said you'd done it at school.

(*Pause.*)

MAM: Anyway, it doesn't do much of a job here, does it?

DAD: What?

MAM: The moon. Tide's never in. Slipping, moon. Bad as the Corporation.

(COLIN *laughs.*)

DAD: Oh ay, that's right. Don't believe me. You make them laugh at me, don't you? Well I'm not going to say aught.

Their thick father. (*Pause.*) Their thick, unemployed
father. You believe me, don't you, Jennifer?

JENNIFER: What?

DAD: About the moon.

JENNIFER: Wasn't listening. I'm cold.

35. EXT. BEACH. DAY

COLIN: I'm bored. (*Pause.*) I'm bored, Dad. (*Pause.*) Dad. I'm
bored.

DAD: You're 12 years old.

COLIN: I am.

DAD: It's grown-ups that are bored. You're having the time of
your life.

COLIN: I'm bored.

DAD: Well, if you're bored now, you'll be more bored when
you're grown up. It gets more boring as you go on.

MAM: You bore me.

COLIN: You bore me.
(DAD *clouts him.*)

MAM: Jack!

DAD: I don't care. Saying that. We come away on holiday and
then he's the cheek to say he's bored.
(COLIN *goes off at this point.*)

MAM: I am getting old arms. My arms. Getting to look right
old.

DAD: Why single out your arms?

MAM: Well, I notice you haven't got into your costume.

DAD: Why should I? Who is there to impress?

MAM: Impress! With that belly?

DAD: I impressed you once.

MAM: Ay. You did. You did that. Funny, we've never been to
Filey since.

JENNIFER: I'm cold.

MAM: If you say you're cold once more, young lady, I'll think of
something to warm you up.

93

DAD: Come here, love.
   (JENNIFER *sits on his knee*.)

36. EXT. BEACH. DAY

MAM: I don't like watching TV in a roomful of folk. (*Pause*.) Do
   you?

DAD: Do I what?

MAM: Like watching with people you don't know.

DAD: It's all right. *Match of the Day*.

MAM: It's not the same as watching it on our own. I'd rather go
   to the proper pictures. I hate being sat there with a jorem of
   folks not knowing what they're like, wondering what
   they're all thinking. (*Pause*.) Plays. I can't watch plays
   among strangers. They have to be people I know.
   Preferably the immediate family. (*Pause*.) You can't talk to
   it.

DAD: What?

MAM: The TV. I like to talk to it.

DAD: Don't start talking to it up there or they'll think you're
   barmy.

MAM: Everybody talks to it. Acts daft. If they're on their own,
   and they think nobody's watching. I do.

DAD: I don't.
   (*Pause*.)

MAM: You're not your own master. Where Dugdales stayed, the
   Clarendon, that has TV in every bedroom. Shower and TV.
   "Private hotel." It's not a proper private hotel. It's not even
   that clean. (*Pause*.) That pillow had hairs on it.

DAD: My hairs.

MAM: They weren't your hairs. I know your hairs. I should
   know your hairs by now. Your hairs aren't like that. They
   were somebody else's hairs. Little curly ones. I found
   another one there this morning.

DAD: They won't kill you. The army, we never even had
   pillowcases. Hairs.

(*Pause.*)

MAM: I think it's that that's stopping me sleeping.

DAD: What?

MAM: Them little hairs. I've not had a proper night since we came. Let alone anything else.

DAD: Well, whose fault is that?

MAM: No. I mean the other. At home I always go like clockwork.

DAD: You said the same at Marbella.

MAM: No, I was the other way at Marbella.

DAD: It's the water.

MAM: It's partly the water. But I'm not struck on that toilet. I don't like them low suites.

DAD: Go to one of the other ones.

MAM: It's half a mile. They're like everything else these days, designed for what it looks like. Whereas we're not. We're not designed for what it looks like, are we?

DAD: What?

MAM: Bottoms!

DAD: Lil! I don't know. We come away on holiday and you get right unsavoury. Toilets. Read the paper.

37. EXT. BEACH. DAY

JENNIFER: Dad. Dad.

MAM: Jennifer.

JENNIFER: Dad.

DAD: What?

JENNIFER: Do you like it here?

MAM: Jennifer.

DAD: Why?

JENNIFER: It's cold. The sea's not blue. It's blue abroad.

MAM: I've told you not to talk about abroad. Your father doesn't want to know about abroad. You're lucky to have been abroad. We'd never been abroad at your age. Abroad. We only came on this holiday for you.

DAD: I don't know why we did. When you reckon it all up there's not much difference in price. That place isn't cheap for what you get. And I'm always hungry.

MAM: You pay for him on that radio, that's what you pay for. (*Pause.*) Do you think that couple at the little table are married?

DAD: Not if he's any sense.

38. EXT. SEASHORE. DAY

COLIN *wanders down through the people sitting on the sands, out into the bay, trying to walk to the edge of the sea. Miles and miles of empty sand. The beach is very small and distant behind him. The very faint sound of the beach. Finally he reaches the edge of the sea. But he isn't sure whether it really is the edge, it's so gradual and undramatic.*

He is called back by shouts of "Colin!"

39. EXT. BEACH. DAY

DAD *gets out the plastic boxes they have brought from the boarding house. "Your Eats" is written on the top of the boxes.*

DAD: "Your Eats." Here, Colin, "Your Eats." "Your Eats."

MAM: What's yours?

DAD: Ham, I think.

MAM: Ham.

DAD: There's a broad bean in mine. D'you ever hear of a sandwich with a broad bean in it? What sort of a sandwich is that? And all these doll's knives and forks. If they spent a bit more on the food and a bit less on what you're supposed to eat it with. Look, individual salt and peppers.
(*He flings them into the sand.*)

COLIN: Litter. Dad. Litter. Mrs Monkman at school says litter's a crime. Mrs Monkman says people ought to be put in prison for dropping litter.
(COLIN *goes and picks up the salt and pepper and puts them back in the box.*)

DAD: Now you've gone and got all sand in the box, you silly little sod. What does Mrs Monkman say about that?

MAM: Don't call Colin a little sod. Calling your own son a sod.

DAD: He's my son. I call him what I want.

MAM: It's all to do with airlines. That's what's done all that. It all has to be like airlines now. All this plastic cutlery. Little salt and pepper. It's pretend we're on an aeroplane.

JENNIFER: I wish we were on an aeroplane.

DAD: Shut up.

MAM: Yes. You lost your sandal. Like trains. They have this voice telling you how fast you're going and there are buffet-car facilities available on this train. It's all splother. All of a sudden everything has to be such a performance. "Your Eats." And one scrutty little apple.

DAD: Ay. If this is the ordinary one God knows what the weight-watchers get. I've finished mine. Look out. The vultures are gathering.

(*He throws stuff to the seagulls.*)

COLIN: Mam.

MAM: What?

COLIN: I want something hot. Can I have something hot?

DAD: Eat them. We've paid for them.

COLIN: Can I not have a pizza?

DAD: No, you can't have a pizza.

COLIN: Mam.

DAD: I said no. You can't have a pizza.

MAM: Anyway, where can you get a pizza?

COLIN: We passed a place. On the front.

DAD: And who's going to pay for it? It's want, want, want. We've got nothing coming in now, you know. You still think your Dad's made of money. They don't give you hand-outs for pizzas.

JENNIFER: I don't. I don't want a pizza.

COLIN: You lost your sandal.

(MAM *gives him some money from her purse.*)

MAM: Here, love.

(COLIN *goes*.)

Well, it's their holidays. Pizzas. We never had pizzas, did we? Still, it's only cheese on toast. It's Welsh rarebit really. Except pizzas are round and Welsh rarebit's square. All that's new as well.

(*Pause.* DAD *stares gloomily out to sea*.)

What's matter?

DAD: Nowt.

MAM: You'll find something when we get back. It's on the turn now. They all say that. It's in the paper.

(*She settles down with the paper, occasionally reading out headlines as* DAD *dozes off*.)

"Blackburn gripped by bread hysteria."

"Pensioner cleared of teacake theft."

"Pope braves drizzle."

40. EXT. BEACH. DAY

Much of the conversation between MAM *and* DAD *in the deckchairs is quite pausey, often because he is half-asleep. This exchange is done very slowly with lots of gaps.*

MAM: Dad.

DAD: What?

MAM: Was it tomato, them sandwiches we had at Rhyl?

DAD: When?

MAM: We had some right nice sandwiches once. Just after we were married. At Rhyl. Were they tomato?

DAD: I don't know.

MAM: I don't know either.

PART TWO

A stone pier on the front. Men fishing. A coin in the slot telescope.
Two old men are sitting on a seat in the sun.

HARRY: I was going to have my hair cut this week. I should
  have gone last week. It'll have to wait while next week now,
  I'm that busy.
ALBERT: Where do you go now?
HARRY: A little fellow on Duncan Street.
ALBERT: Duncan Street?
HARRY: Ay. Little Indian feller on Duncan Street. Next to the
  confectioner's.
ALBERT: Dear do now, haircut. How much do they charge?
HARRY: 60p.
ALBERT: 60p? By – ! It's shocking.
HARRY: I used to go on East Parade. Mr Batty. I went in there
  one morning and there's a bloody lass having her hair done.
  I said, "What's this?" The lad says, "We've gone unisex." I
  says, "Unisex? Where's Mr Batty, then?" He says,
  "Retired." I says, "Retired? He was only about 14."
  "Well," he says, "he's in Garstang. Furthermore," he says,
  "what with the expense of going unisex, we have been
  compelled to withdraw our concessions to pensioners." I
  came away.
ALBERT: They want reporting.
HARRY: What do they want with unisex in Morecambe?
ALBERT: It's like these sauna baths. They're popping up all over
  now. Sauna baths. Who's going to patronize sauna baths in
  Morecambe? Folk aren't coming to Morecambe for sauna
  baths.

(COLIN *comes up*.)

COLIN: Can you change 10p, please?

ALBERT: What do you want it for?

COLIN: 5p for the telescope.

ALBERT: No. I can't. Here. Here's 5p. I'll treat you.

COLIN: Ta.

ALBERT: (*Calling after him*) What're you wanting to see? T'sea?

HARRY: You shouldn't have given him that. He'll only look at the lasses on the beach.

ALBERT: He's too young for that.

HARRY: There's no too young nowadays. They start at 10 year old.

ALBERT: I wished I'd have started at 10. I were wed at 17.

HARRY: Ay.

(ALBERT *gets up and goes over to* COLIN *and the telescope*.)

ALBERT: Let's have a look. (*He peers through*.) By – ! That's marvellous. Oh. T'beggar's clicked off. Short do.

42. EXT. BEACH. DAY

MAM *and* DAD *are both asleep*.

JENNIFER: Mam. Mam. *Mam*.

MAM: What?

JENNIFER: Take us for a paddle.

MAM: It's miles.

JENNIFER: Go on, Mam.

(*The two of them begin to walk towards the sea. It is a long long way over the wet sand*.)

43. EXT. SEASHORE. DAY

MAM: Morecambe is where your Dad and me did our courting.

JENNIFER: I liked Benidorm.

MAM: There's no question of Benidorm now.

JENNIFER: I liked it.

(*They have come to the water's edge*.)

Is this the sea?

MAM: I think so.

JENNIFER: Where are the cliffs?

MAM: There aren't cliffs here.

JENNIFER: The book said cliffs.

MAM: Not at Morecambe. This is the water's edge.

JENNIFER: Is this the proper sea?

MAM: Yes.

JENNIFER: Paddle with me.

MAM: I am paddling with you.

JENNIFER: Paddle in the sea.

(*They do so. Then turn and walk on the sands. Suddenly a sand yacht passes, with a* YOUNG MAN *on it, brown and beautiful and laughing. It should be wonderful, like something out of a television commercial. It is a vision.*)

MAM: Mustn't that be wonderful?

JENNIFER: Can we go on one?

MAM: No. We'd better go back. Your Dad will be wondering where we've got to.

44. INT. ICE-CREAM PARLOUR. DAY

A timid-looking MAN *is waiting. The* WOMAN *is a long time coming.* COLIN *is waiting behind the* MAN.

MAN: What sort is there?

WOMAN: There's strawberry, raspberry, vanilla, chocolate peppermint, caramel and blackcurrant.

MAN: Is there coffee?

WOMAN: (*Calling to another waitress*) Gloria. It's going to be one of those days.

45. EXT. STREET. DAY

Cut to COLIN *walking along eating ice-cream.*

46. EXT. PIZZA PARLOUR/FISHING-LINE SHOP. DAY

COLIN *looks at the money he has left. He hesitates outside the pizza parlour. Then goes into a shop selling fishing lines. He comes out*

without one. He looks at the fishing lines on display. The
SHOPKEEPER *comes and stands in the doorway watching him.*
COLIN *walks on.*

47. EXT. BOATING POOL. DAY

A middle-aged MAN *is sailing a motor yacht. He sails it towards
him.* COLIN *watches him. Then walks round to meet it. Another*
BOY *is also watching.*

MAN: (*Who speaks without looking at him*) Would you like to
    work it? Are you mechanically minded?

COLIN: Yes. No.

MAN: Fancy being a sailor? I've got a whole fleet at home. Isn't
    she beautiful? What's your name?

COLIN: Colin.

MAN: What's your friend's name?
    (COLIN *looks at the other boy,* GRAHAM.)

COLIN: I don't know. He's not with me.
    (COLIN *sets its course across the pool and the three of them walk
    round to meet it.*)

GRAHAM: Let's have a go then.
    (*He winks at* COLIN *behind the* MAN'S *back and sets the course
    of the boat straight for a breakwater, which it hits and turns
    over.*)

MAN: Don't do that. What did you do that for?

GRAHAM: What're you laking with boats for, you? You're as old
    as my Dad.
    (*He walks away with* COLIN.)
    He's a queer. He's always there. He's been had up. (*Shouts*)
    Poof!

48. EXT. BATHING HUTS. DAY

COLIN *and* GRAHAM *are behind a row of bathing huts.* GRAHAM *is
going along, looking in spy-holes in the back of the huts. He beckons
to* COLIN *to look.*

COLIN: She's old.

GRAHAM: She's bare. Can you see it?
COLIN: No.
GRAHAM: Let's see. I can. I saw it.
COLIN: Let's see.
GRAHAM: She's got her cossie on now.
   (*They peep at the* WOMAN *as she comes out in her bathing costume.*)
GRAHAM: It's when two go in you want to be there.
COLIN: Yes.
GRAHAM: I've seen that. Fantastic. What's your name?
COLIN: Colin. What's yours?
GRAHAM: Graham.

49. EXT. JETTY. DAY
COLIN *and* GRAHAM *are walking along the jetty. There are people fishing. They watch them, catching nothing.*
GRAHAM: It's boring, fishing. Fishing's boring. Fastening it on, taking it off. Waiting. It's boring.
   (*They walk on.*)

50. EXT. JETTY. DAY
GRAHAM: What you want a fishing line for?
COLIN: I've lost something.
GRAHAM: You want to nick one.
COLIN: No.
GRAHAM: Yes.
COLIN: Who off?

51. EXT. JETTY. DAY
Cut to a BOY *crying, running down the jetty.* COLIN *and* GRAHAM *running away,* COLIN *trailing a line and winding it up as he runs.*

52. EXT. BOARDING HOUSE. DAY
Cut to COLIN *approaching the boarding house. Entering the front*

door very cautiously. There is no one about, but a distant sound of talking from the back room. He goes upstairs.

53. INT. BOARDING HOUSE: COLIN'S AND JENNIFER'S ROOM. DAY

COLIN *opens the window. The shoe is still lying on the flat roof below.*

54. INT. BOARDING HOUSE: CATTLEYS' ROOM. DAY

Cut to landlady's room. MR *and* MRS CATTLEY. *Long pause.*

MR CATTLEY: It's not a man's job. Sitting in the launderette. They're all women. Apart from me. Washing sheets. I won't go.

MRS CATTLEY: If you don't, I'm cutting off your intercommunication system. "The Portofino Room is now open for the service of high tea." What's wrong with a gong? I can remember when I used to shout up the stairs.

MR CATTLEY: They won't take that now. Shouting up the stairs. Gongs. You have to have that Riviera feel.

MRS CATTLEY: Listen we're half-empty. So much for the Riviera feel.

MR CATTLEY: Everywhere's half-empty this year. It's down all over.

(*He sees a child's shoe slowly ascending outside the window.*)

Denise.

(*He touches her arm.*)

MRS CATTLEY: Don't Denise me. And none of that either. I don't want any of that. There's too much of that goes on in this place. No wonder we're running to the launderette every five minutes.

MR CATTLEY: Denise.

(*She looks.*)

55. INT. BOARDING HOUSE: COLIN'S AND JENNIFER'S BEDROOM. DAY

COLIN: It's our Jennifer's shoe. It fell out of the window.

MRS CATTLEY: Fell? Chucked, more like. Why didn't you ask us for it? We have access to the roof.

MR CATTLEY: Ask us for it, that's right. Access, no problem.

COLIN: I didn't think.

MRS CATTLEY: Didn't your mother think?

MR CATTLEY: Didn't she think? We're not inhuman, are we, Denise?

MRS CATTLEY: That could go through the double glazing. And do you know what that is? Two hundred pounds down the drain.

MR CATTLEY: It could go in somebody's eye. And what does the Insurance say then? "Fishing for sandals outside the bedroom window. Not covered by the policy, Mr Cattley. Not in the small print."

56. INT. BOARDING HOUSE: CORRIDOR/STAIRS. DAY

They are coming out of the bedroom and coming downstairs.

MRS CATTLEY: Yes, all right, Percy. Where does your Mam think you are?

COLIN: I don't know.

MRS CATTLEY: Well, I shall tell her.

MR CATTLEY: I shall tell her.

MRS CATTLEY: I'll tell her, Percy. Why aren't you out enjoying yourself, instead of being stuck inside fishing for sandals? I'm keeping this to give to your mother.

COLIN: It's our Jennifer's.

MR CATTLEY: We shall give it to your mother. Show her what you've been up to.

COLIN: She's only got that pair. She can't have another pair. My Dad's . . .

MRS CATTLEY: Your Dad's what?

COLIN: My Dad says.

MR CATTLEY: Your Dad says, why?

MRS CATTLEY: What's the matter with your Dad?

COLIN: Nothing.

MR CATTLEY: What about him?

MRS CATTLEY: What is it?

COLIN: Nothing. He's out of work.

    (*He breaks free and runs off down the stairs and out. The* HONEYMOON COUPLE *are coming upstairs – past the* CATTLEYS.)

KEITH: She's got a headache.

JO: I've got a headache.

57. INT. BOARDING HOUSE: KITCHEN. DAY

MRS CATTLEY: Out of work and coming on holiday. That's not going to get the country back on its feet. Losing shoes.

MR CATTLEY: He could just have told me. There would have been no problem. I could have broadcast an appeal.

MRS CATTLEY: Out of work. That's the sort of clientele *we* get. That's your "Riviera feel".

58. EXT. BEACH. DAY

The tide is coming in and the beach has got more crowded. COLIN *gets back just as the family are beginning to pack up.*

MAM: Where've you been?

COLIN: Nowhere.

DAD: Carry this then. Jennifer. Come on.

    (JENNIFER *kicks over her sand-castle before going.*)

59. EXT. PROMENADE. DAY

MR *and* MRS THORNTON *are sitting on the prom. They are chatting to the* COOPERS.

MR THORNTON: No, we haven't done much. We had a little look round Marks and Spencer's, then we sat in a shelter for a bit. We thought we'd take it easy today since we're going to Grange tomorrow.

DAD: You do right.

MRS THORNTON: It's all so hectic. Even Morecambe. I've watched this place get hectic. It's going to be like the South of France soon.

MR THORNTON: There's a hell-hole. Course you generally go
there.

(*They get up and walk along the prom with* MAM *and* DAD *and*
JENNIFER.)

MAM: It's been more Spain. But I think you're right, Spain's
spoilt now. It's been an eye-opener to me, this holiday. You
can have just as good a time at home.

MR THORNTON: That's right. Holidays at Home.

DAD: Colin. Keep up. Come on.

(*There is another family walking ahead of them. It is the boy,*
DEREK, *whose fishing line* COLIN *has taken.* COLIN *has seen*
him. DEREK *looks round. Says something to his* FATHER. *The*
FATHER *looks back.* DEREK *looks back again. He stops and*
they catch up.)

DEREK'S FATHER: Is this your lad?

DAD: Which? Colin? Yes. Why?

DEREK'S FATHER: Does he generally thieve, then?

DAD: Thieve?

DEREK'S FATHER: Thieve. Nick. Lift.

DAD: How do you mean, thieve?

MAM: Dad, what's the matter?

DEREK'S FATHER: He pinched our Derek's fishing line, didn't
he, Derek?

DEREK: Him and another one. The other one hit me.

MAM: Well, we don't have another one.

(*The* THORNTONS *listen to this exchange.*)

MRS THORNTON: (*Mouthing*) We'll go on.

(*The* THORNTONS *leave.*)

DEREK'S FATHER: He says it was him.

DEREK: Yes.

COLIN: I didn't.

DEREK'S FATHER: He says he did.

DAD: Well, he says he didn't.

DEREK'S FATHER: Look in his pockets.

DAD: Look in your pockets.

COLIN: I've looked in my pockets.

DAD: Look again.

DEREK'S FATHER: Let me look in his pockets.

DAD: Don't you touch him.

DEREK'S FATHER: Well, I don't know.

(*One mother smiles uneasily at the other mother, both somewhat embarrassed and not knowing what to do.*)

He's not that sort of a lad.

DAD: Nor is our Colin. You're sure?

COLIN: Course I'm sure.

DEREK'S MOTHER: Well, come on then. It may not be him.

DEREK: It is him.

DEREK'S MOTHER: Shut up. Flaming fishing line.

60. EXT. ROAD TO BOARDING HOUSE. DAY

They continue back to the digs. Much of this shot on COLIN's *face.*

MOTHER: That kid. Telling t'tale. He was just trying it on.
"Look in his pockets." I'd have clouted him. Going up to
people in the street. Fishing. He was fishing. That's what
he was doing. Then showing us up in front of Mr and Mrs
Thornton. You'll have to tell them it was all a mistake or
it'll be all over the digs.

DAD: Never heed. Kids. I don't know.

61. INT. BOARDING HOUSE: HALL/STAIRS. DAY

They go into the hall of the boarding house, and begin to go upstairs.
Two flights. Slowly. As they get to the bedroom, the Tannoy goes.)

MR CATTLEY: (*Over the Tannoy*) Would Mr Cooper please come
to Reception. Mr Cooper to Reception, please.

(DAD *turns and goes down again.*)

62. INT. BOARDING HOUSE: COLIN'S AND JENNIFER'S
BEDROOM. DAY

COLIN *is alone in the bedroom.*

DAD: (*Out of vision*) Colin. Colin.
COLIN: What?

63. INT. BOARDING HOUSE: LANDING OUTSIDE COLIN'S AND
JENNIFER'S BEDROOM. DAY
DAD: Open me this door. Open me this door.
    (MAM *is at the head of the stairs watching.*)
COLIN: (*Out of vision*) I won't.
DAD: You will. You bloody well will.
MAM: Dad.
    (DAD *gets up on a chair and looks impotently through the glass
    pane above the door. He gets down and goes away.*)

64. INT. BOARDING HOUSE: COLIN'S AND JENNIFER'S
BEDROOM. DAY
A little knock on the door.
JENNIFER: (*Out of vision*) Colin. Can I come in?
COLIN: No.
JENNIFER: (*Out of vision*) Go on.
DAD: (*Out of vision, whispering*) Say you want your Teddy.
JENNIFER: (*Out of vision*) I want my Teddy.
COLIN: Bugger Teddy.
JENNIFER: (*Out of vision*) Go on. Colin. Go on.

65. INT. BOARDING HOUSE: LANDING OUTSIDE COLIN'S AND
JENNIFER'S BEDROOM. DAY
COLIN *opens it. It is instantly pushed open.* DAD *springs in and
starts hitting him.* MAM *waits on the half-landing below, hearing but
not seeing.*
MAM: Dad, Dad. Don't hit him on his head, Dad.
DAD: Showing us up. I'll give you fishing line. Why didn't you
    say? All you have to do is say. The sandal dropped out of
    the window. Full stop. Can we get it? Full stop. Stead of
    which you go pinching fishing lines, and spreading it
    around I'm unemployed. Well, I'm employed now, doing

something useful for a change.

(KEITH *comes out, half-dressed, and comes up the stairs.*)

Yes?

KEITH: Nothing. I just wondered what was going on.

DAD: Nothing's going on. Family life's going on. Happily ever after's going on. Marriage. Kids. That's what's going on.

KEITH: Sorry.

DAD: Just got married, have you? Magic, is it? Bliss? Well, take a good look, because you'll come to it before you know where you are. And don't you be looking so suited, our Jennifer, or I'll fetch you one and all. Flaming sandal. You make life more complicated. We're trying to make life easy and you're making it more complicated. Get in there.

(*He flings* COLIN *into the bedroom and shuts the door on him.*)

66. INT. BOARDING HOUSE: COLIN'S AND JENNIFER'S BEDROOM. DAY

COLIN *lies on the bed, crying.*

67. INT. BOARDING HOUSE: PORTOFINO ROOM. DAY

The dining room is empty apart from FAY. *And the happy couple – the older woman, the young man –* HILDA *and* LESLIE, *sitting by the window.*

MR CATTLEY: (*Over the Tannoy*) . . . for starters, orange juice, grapefruit juice, grapefruit segments or melon balls, followed by duck à l'orange, fresh Norfolk peas and sauté potatoes. For afters we have a second chance to sample Mrs Cattley's famous home-made trifle, plus wafer-thin mints and a choice of beverages.

68. INT. BOARDING HOUSE: COLIN'S AND JENNIFER'S BEDROOM. DAY

COLIN *is sitting by the window, looking out over the roofs and through the chimney-pots and television aerials to the distant glitter which is the sea.*

ONE FINE DAY

CHARACTERS

WELBY

BLAKE

STEELE

MARSH

BLOUNT

PHILLIPS

RYCROFT

MISS VENABLES

AVRIL

SANDRA

CHRISTINE

FIRST MAN IN LIFT

SECOND MAN IN LIFT

THIRD MAN IN LIFT

MRS PHILLIPS

JENNIFER

ROBIN PHILLIPS

COMMISSIONAIRE

MISS MORPETH

WOMAN IN KEY SHOP

LINDA

ARNOLD

MILTON

MR ALPERT

JAPANESE CLIENT

YOUNG MAN ON ROOF

YOUNG WOMAN ON ROOF

JUNE

One Fine Day was first transmitted by London Weekend Television on 17 February 1979. The cast included:

WELBY	Robert Stephens
BLAKE	Benjamin Whitrow
STEELE	Edward de Souza
MARSH	Toby Salaman
BLOUNT	Harold Innocent
PHILLIPS	Dave Allen
RYCROFT	Dominic Guard
MISS VENABLES	Joan Scott
AVRIL	Mary Maddox
SANDRA	Liz Crowther
CHRISTINE	Sheila Kelley
FIRST MAN IN LIFT	Hugh Fraser
SECOND MAN IN LIFT	Bill Paterson
THIRD MAN IN LIFT	Gregory Floy
MRS PHILLIPS	Barbara Leigh-Hunt
JENNIFER	Madeleine Church
ROBIN PHILLIPS	Patrick Bailey
COMMISSIONAIRE	Leslie Sands
MISS MORPETH	Rosamund Greenwood
LINDA	Suzanna Hamilton
ARNOLD	Don Fellows
MILTON	Bruce Boa
MR ALPERT	Anthony Sher
Producer and Director	Stephen Frears
Designer	Frank Nerini
Music	George Fenton

PART ONE

1. INT. FROBISHER, RENDELL & ROSS: BOARDROOM. DAY

The offices of a large London estate agents. A dozen or so men sitting round a long table. It is towards the end of a meeting and the table is strewn with papers. Briefcases by their chairs. Much of the meeting shot from the point of view of PHILLIPS, *a man in his late forties.* WELBY, *the Chairman, is turning over various folders.*

WELBY: What about Fordyce Road? Have we had any feedback there?

BLAKE: The odd nibble. No real joy to speak of.

STEELE: I think Fordyce Road is maybe a sleeper.

MARSH: It's certainly that.

(*There is **uneasy laughter** which* WELBY *silences with a wide smile.*)

BLAKE: No, seriously, Charles, *au sujet de* Fordyce Road, I think you may find me coming back to you round about Wednesday.

STEELE: Hint, hint.

BLAKE: The odd feeler, you know.

WELBY: Jolly good. Joll–ll–y good. Well, Charles, we'll keep everything crossed on that one, shall we? (*Turns over more folders.*) Compass House. We've done all . . . that. Contracts exchanged . . . when did you say, Rupert?

BLOUNT: Tuesday.

WELBY: Tuesday, Tuesday, Tuesday. Charles on Tuesday. Maurice on Wednesday. It's all happening, isn't it? Jolly good. Ah. Here's the bluebottle in the vaseline. Our old friend. Sunley House. (*He has a brochure of the building with a photograph.*) Any glad tidings there, George?

(PHILLIPS *shakes his head.*)

Glad – ish?

PHILLIPS: Not as such.

WELBY: Not as such. I see. That's a pity. Because this is the big one.

MARSH: It's the big one, all right.

WELBY: How long have we had it in the window? A year, is it?

MARSH: More like two.

WELBY: Two . . . years. One appreciates it's only lately been your pigeon, George, but, you see, what one is . . . a little . . . worried about . . . I say worried, do I mean worried? Yes, I think I do mean worried . . . what one is worried about, George, is that it's getting to look a fraction flyblown. Starting to curl at the edge a bit. Know what I mean?

PHILLIPS: Sort of.

(*Pause.*)

WELBY: Would it help if we could locate the difficulty?

PHILLIPS: Lockwood found the same.

WELBY: Lockwood was a sick man.

MARSH: It's a prime location.

PHILLIPS: Oh, sure, it's a prime location.

WELBY: Poor Lockwood used to say we would never rent Sunley House until the bottoming out. Well, we've had the bottoming out. We had it eighteen months ago. But we're still stuck with Sunley House. Now why, George? I'm genuinely puzzled.

PHILLIPS: There is a backlog. Still some highly rentable properties that have been held over. The slack is still in process of being taken up. Our turn will come.

WELBY: Turn? Turn, George? You're not suggesting we *wait* our turn?

(*Pause. He makes this remark a joke – though it isn't a joke – smiling widely at the board meeting, who smile back.*)

Moreover I was reading in the Pink 'un this morning that there *is* no slack. The commercial sector is poised. Taut. The crest, as it were, of the wave.

RYCROFT: (*An attractive young man of 25*) Yes. I was reading that.

WELBY: I once heard Lockwood . . . admittedly it was when he was a very sick man . . . I once heard Lockwood refer to it as "White Elephant House". That shocked me, George. Deeply shocked me. And I am wondering if his attitudes haven't, as it were . . . carried over.

PHILLIPS: I am sure it will find its own slot, in time.

WELBY: In time. In time. I just wish I had your philosophy, George. Your Gaelic philosophy. Time. Hey ho!

RYCROFT: Could Residential have a crack at it? If Commercial don't mind, that is.

(PHILLIPS *deliberately pours water into a glass and shows no sign of answering.*)

WELBY: What say, George?

PHILLIPS: It's not been designed for unit occupancy. It was put up in the palmy days when you built first and found a tenant afterwards. Then the money ran out, so the top floor is a shambles.

WELBY: Don't show them the top floor.

PHILLIPS: I don't. (*Pause.*) Who wants 80,000 square feet of that sort of office space nowadays?

MARSH: Our Middle East friends, for a start.

WELBY: Quite. All I would say is that I don't think in all honesty there is any point in any of us just sitting on our backsides waiting for the economic climate to do the job for us. The index is on the up and up. Records are being broken, North Sea oil or no North Sea oil, the country is well and truly back on its feet. But we can't sit back. We can't be passengers. It's firms like us that are making that happen. We can't just wait our turn? Time . . . (*Slightly mimicking* PHILLIPS) . . . time . . . is of the essence. And that, since it's now after the witching hour of four thirty, is the message I think we ought to carry away with us. Gentlemen.

WELBY *chats to* RYCROFT *at the door, obviously waiting to have a word with* PHILLIPS, *who lingers. The other men come out, nodding and smiling as they come past* WELBY *and the room empties.*

RYCROFT: Hope I wasn't out of order on that one, sir.

WELBY: Absolutely not, Rycroft. Absolutely not. That's what these meetings are for. A monthly powwow. Protocol gets left at the door. Commercial, Residential. Your patch, my patch. Nonsense. The firm, Gerald. Selling. Business. That's what matters. What are toes for but to be trod on? Quite right to speak up.

(WELBY *is seen talking from* PHILLIPS's *point of view, as* PHILLIPS *still lingers. To avoid going out he examines a picture on the wall.*)

PHILLIPS: What is that, precisely?

STEELE: It's not meant to be anything in particular, is it? One of these abstract jobs.

PHILLIPS: Abstract what, though? You like it?

STEELE: I'm not frantic about it. Actually I've never really looked at it before.

(*He gets interested.*)

PHILLIPS: Nor me. I'd say . . . it was probably rubbish.

(WELBY *appears to have gone so* PHILLIPS *follows* STEELE *out.*)

2. INT. FROBISHER, RENDELL & ROSS: CORRIDOR. DAY

PHILLIPS *walks along the corridor behind* BLOUNT *and* BLAKE.

BLOUNT: Lambeth have done another nasty.

BLAKE: You surprise me.

BLOUNT: Slapped a 416 on Twyford Street.

BLAKE: Where's Arthur at this crucial juncture?

BLOUNT: Swindon.

BLAKE: It never rains. So what's the plan?

BLOUNT: No plan. A 416? No *plan.*

BLAKE: And where's Arthur?

BLOUNT: Swindon.

BLAKE: Of course. Well, it's the big decision.

BLOUNT: What?

BLAKE: Does he put his head in the gas oven there or come back here and do it?

MISS VENABLES: (*She has a tray of flags.*) Can I hold you to ransom? For kidney patients. Dialysis. A wonderful cause. (WELBY *has been waiting in a doorway half-way down the corridor, talking to* MARSH. *He breaks off instantly to capture* PHILLIPS *as he passes. He walks along the corridor with him.*)

WELBY: My worry is, George, that so long as we've got this place on our hands it will go on distorting the quarterly estimates.

PHILLIPS: I appreciate that.

WELBY: I think you do appreciate that. I think you do appreciate it. But I don't want Central to run away with the impression we're dragging our feet over this one. At the same time I don't want to have to spell it out then have Glover ringing up saying, "Sorry, no understand problem." You've got acres of room leasewise. When you think what we're forking out in interest alone, nobody's going to complain if you come right down. I'm not suggesting you do come right down, but if it gets it off our hands . . . (*Awkward silence.*)

Anyway . . . How are things on the family front? Elizabeth well?

PHILLIPS: Fine.

WELBY: How are the lampshades?

PHILLIPS: Conversational Spanish now.

WELBY: That's interesting.

3. INT. FROBISHER, RENDELL & ROSS: OUTER OFFICE/PHILLIPS'S OFFICE. DAY
Three secretaries, CHRISTINE, SANDRA *and* AVRIL, *at three desks.* CHRISTINE *is on the phone.*

AVRIL: Well, a daiquiri basically is lime juice, Bacardi rum,

sugar and a dash of maraschino. Only that's really only the
bare essentials. The art is what you put into it besides.
When I was in Corfu with Lynne we had cherry daiquiris.
(SANDRA's *phone rings*.)

SANDRA: I don't dislike Riesling. Have you had that? Frobisher,
Rendell and Ross . . . I rather think Mr Welby is in a
meeting at this moment . . .
(*At this point*, WELBY *and* PHILLIPS *come in*.)
Hang on, I'll just check. (*Mouthing at* WELBY) Mr
Crookshank.
(WELBY *pulls a face and shakes his head*.)
No, I'm afraid he's in a meeting . . . He'll be tied up now
for the rest of the afternoon. Does he have your number?
. . . Goodbye.
(CHRISTINE's *conversation on the phone should be heard only
in the background*.)

CHRISTINE: Brenda said I was a fool and was he index-linked?
Well, I never asked but you can't go building your life on
somebody else's pension prospects, can you? But I think
you're right about beards. I mean they were all right when
they were just starting, but now everybody's got them
they've lost their distinction.
(WELBY *and* PHILLIPS *appear*.)
Hold on just one second.
(*She puts her hand over the phone and waits for* WELBY *to go*.)

WELBY: Rycroft's a bright spark, isn't he? I like him. I like
him. Well. These things are sent to try us. Press on. Press
on. (*He smiles at the typists*.) Don't tell me. Don't tell me.
Miss . . . (*searches for* AVRIL's *name*) Williamson, no, as you
were, as you were . . . Hopkins . . . ?
(AVRIL *turns round the name card on her desk. It is Hopkins*.)
Where's Miss Williamson now? Reading?

AVRIL: Cirencester.

WELBY: Cirencester!
(*He goes away smiling*. CHRISTINE, PHILLIPS's *secretary, is*

still on the telephone. We see PHILLIPS *pass her and take some papers she hands him without stopping talking. The scene is shot on* PHILLIPS.)

CHRISTINE: (*Out of vision*) Are you still there? No. He keeps threatening to take me to this topless steak-house. Aylesbury. And he makes out that's a treat for *me*. Besides it's so old-fashioned. People don't go on about topless now. It's really sixties is topless. He's a bit sixties actually. I like him but he is sixties. Stuart. It's a sixties name. A little Fiaty thing. I think. Else it's a Renault. I don't know about cars. Red. Calls it Clarence. Not sure I like that. It's a bit silly studenty. No. Works for the council. Anyway, Mr Phillips has just come in . . . my lord and master . . . yes . . . just entered. I'd better dash. Yes. No. Don't work too hard.

(PHILLIPS *signs the papers. Reads and signs. Reads and signs. Gives them to* CHRISTINE.)

PHILLIPS: That it?

CHRISTINE: Cheer up.

PHILLIPS: I'm all right. End of the day.

(*He gets his coat from the stand and goes out.*)

4. INT. FROBISHER, RENDELL & ROSS: CORRIDOR. DAY

PHILLIPS *goes along the corridor. He passes an office where* MARSH *and* BLOUNT *are checking through a list.*

MARSH: 16 Dickinson Road.

BLOUNT: 16 Dickinson Road.

MARSH: 27 Wadham Gardens.

BLOUNT: 27 Wadham Gardens.

MARSH: 45 Montague Place.

BLOUNT: 45 Montague Place.

MARSH: 2 Queen Mary's Road.

(*Pause.*)

BLOUNT: 2 Queen Mary's Road.

MARSH: Hillcrest, Wilton Avenue.

BLOUNT: Hillcrest, Wilton Avenue.

MARSH: Hewer House. 16 and 17.

BLOUNT: 16 and 17 Hewer House.

> (*And so on, as long as necessary. At some point during this list,*
> BLOUNT *should see* PHILLIPS *pass.*)
> You off?
> (PHILLIPS *nods and raises a hand.*)
> All right for some.
> (*Then he goes on with the list.*)

5. INT. FROBISHER, RENDELL & ROSS: LIFT. DAY

Fairly large and crowded. People staring straight front and watching
the floor indicator. Two MEN *talk in a half undertone. Much of this*
shot on PHILLIPS.

FIRST MAN: Bit of an eccentric apparently. Set off to walk right
   across Europe in a straight line. The Alps, everything.
   Ended up having a paddle in the Mediterranean.

SECOND MAN: Yes? Wish I'd seen that.

> (*The lift stops at a floor. Conversation ceases and starts again*
> *when the lift starts.*)
> Some trek.

FIRST MAN: I'll say.

ANOTHER VOICE: Hit three for me somebody.

FIRST MAN: Of course he wouldn't be on his own.

SECOND MAN: No?

FIRST MAN: You'd have the camera, the producer, the whole
   bag of tricks.

THIRD MAN: (*Getting off*) Gangway! Let the dog see the rabbit.
   (*Lift stops. Conversation stops as before.*)

SECOND MAN: Didn't tempt you, then?

FIRST MAN: What?

SECOND MAN: To set off on your travels?

FIRST MAN: Get out my rucksack.

SECOND MAN: Shorts.

FIRST MAN: I like to think I'm needed.

SECOND MAN: Yes. Break Personnel's heart.
FIRST MAN: Heart!
(*Lift stops and everyone gets off, including* PHILLIPS. *Other faces expressionless or half-smiles.*)

6. EXT. SUNLEY HOUSE. DAY
PHILLIPS *outside a tall office block, which is empty and the forecourt dilapidated. Litter. His car is parked. Some graffiti sprayed on the wall. He peers in. View into the interior of the building from outside. Dim vistas, with reflection from outside. View of* PHILLIPS *from inside the building, looking at it.*

7. INT./EXT. PHILLIPS'S CAR/SUBURBAN COUNTRYISH ROAD. DAY
PHILLIPS *driving home. No other traffic. He brakes hard and stops. Gets out. Goes back. He has run over a hedgehog. He touches it gingerly with his foot, grimacing slightly. It isn't dead.* PHILLIPS *in the car, reversing. He winces as the car goes over it again. Drives forward again. Stops, but doesn't get out. Drives on.*

8. INT. PHILLIPS'S HOME: KITCHEN. EVENING
PHILLIPS *his* WIFE, *a slightly scatty woman in her forties. His son,* ROBIN, *and a silent girl,* JENNIFER. *They are having supper.*
MRS PHILLIPS: It's the pottest of luck, I'm afraid. I was rushing round to get to my class. Does Jennifer want some salad?
(ROBIN *looks at* JENNIFER. JENNIFER *slightly shakes her head.*)
    Apparently Jennifer's father has a market garden.
PHILLIPS: A market garden?
JENNIFER: It's actually more of a nursery than a market garden.
MRS PHILLIPS: I imagine that must be very satisfying. Growing things.
ROBIN: Is it?
JENNIFER: Is it what?
ROBIN: Very satisfying?
JENNIFER: I don't know.

ROBIN: Anybody going to eat this? (*The last potato.*)
MRS PHILLIPS: Offer it to Jennifer.
ROBIN: Jennifer, do you want this?
>(*She mutely shakes her head.*)

A little later in the meal.
PHILLIPS: I ran over a hedgehog tonight.
>(*Pause.*)
MRS PHILLIPS: You see so many killed. I suppose it's their own
>fault. Why do they cross the road?
ROBIN: Why does the hedgehog cross the road!
JENNIFER: They . . .
>(*The table waits.*)
>They have fleas.
ROBIN: How would you know?
JENNIFER: I do know. They have fleas.
PHILLIPS: They do have fleas.
ROBIN: Oh, well, if Dad says so.
JENNIFER: They're smothered in fleas.
>(*Pause.*) I'm doing O level Biology.
MRS PHILLIPS: Shall we stack?

A little later.
MRS PHILLIPS: (*To* ROBIN *and* JENNIFER) Go through. I'll
>bring coffee in.
>(*They are stacking the dishwasher.*)
>It's only a week. Ten days at the most. Father's so difficult
>now, Betty ought to have a break. (*Pause.*) She *is* my sister.
PHILLIPS: I've said. I can manage.
MRS PHILLIPS: You are lucky. Having no parents. Dragging
>on. You don't know you're born. Anyway . . . if I stock up
>the freezer. You can fend. You'll probably rather enjoy it.
PHILLIPS: Probably.
MRS PHILLIPS: It'll mean missing a couple of my classes.
PHILLIPS: That's a pity.

MRS PHILLIPS: I'm really revelling in them now. I thought at
first I wasn't going to, as I didn't like the instructor much
. . . though I suppose he's got a point. He just didn't want
the course cluttered up with well-meaning people.
(*She starts up the coffee grinder so that what she says next is
totally inaudible to* PHILLIPS, *just her mouth moving. Once the
grinding is done she becomes audible again.*)
. . . though as he says, patience is half the battle, and it's
often a matter of just sitting and sitting there while they
puzzle it out, but there does come a point when the
technical training will come in handy, you know. Well, it's
not technical really. Practical, I suppose I mean.
Sympathy's all very well, but teaching is what they want.

PHILLIPS: Sorry. What is this?

MRS PHILLIPS: Dyslexics. People who can't read. There's a
woman there, nice-looking woman, comes in a car. Thirty
probably, 35, hard to tell: she cannot read a word. I said,
"Well, what about the Highway Code?" She said her
husband read it to her and she memorized it. "Bus Stop"
she can recognize, and "Exit" – and that's about all.
Terrible. You never think.

PHILLIPS: Never think what?

MRS PHILLIPS: I don't know. Other people's lives.

PHILLIPS: She seems a nice girl.

MRS PHILLIPS: Who?

PHILLIPS: This girl. Jennifer.

MRS PHILLIPS: Yes. Shy. But I like that.

PHILLIPS: Why does he want to bring her home?

MRS PHILLIPS: It's natural.

PHILLIPS: It's not natural. It's not natural at all. I never did. I
don't want to see her.

MRS PHILLIPS: I think it's nice he feels able to. Rather
touching. I think maybe . . . she's going to stay the night.

PHILLIPS: Where're you putting her? (*Pause.*) Oh, I see.

MRS PHILLIPS: I was supposed to ask you.

PHILLIPS: Why me?

MRS PHILLIPS: If you minded. Do you mind?

PHILLIPS: I don't know. Do you?

MRS PHILLIPS: Doesn't bother me. I mean these days.

PHILLIPS: He's still at school. So is she.

MRS PHILLIPS: I was rather touched him asking. It's probably happened before when we've not been here. I think he just wants us to approve. (*She has the coffee tray ready.*) You coming in?

PHILLIPS: In a minute.

(*She goes in, leaving him sitting there.*)

9. INT. PHILLIPS'S HOME: LOUNGE. NIGHT

A big room. Fairly dark. Pools of light. Stockbroker Tudor.
PHILLIPS *is sitting at one end of the room where there is a stereo. The other three are round the fireplace.* PHILLIPS *has headphones on, so all we can hear is the music in his headphones, while seeing some sort of conversation going on. He is listening to Madame Butterfly. There is some looking over towards his end of the room, and eventually* ROBIN *walks across and stands in front of him saying something, but we just see his lips moving and can't hear.* PHILLIPS *takes the headphones off.*

PHILLIPS: Sorry?

ROBIN: We were just saying goodnight, Dad.

PHILLIPS: Oh. Yes. Goodnight. Goodnight.

(*The second goodnight is to* JENNIFER *who is waiting unselfconsciously near the door. The* BOY *and* GIRL *go, while* MRS PHILLIPS *sits smiling placidly on the sofa, and* PHILLIPS *stares into space, the sound of the opera coming tinnily through the headphones on his lap.*)

10. INT. PHILLIPS'S HOME: BEDROOM. NIGHT

PHILLIPS *and* MRS PHILLIPS *are getting ready for bed.*

PHILLIPS: Doesn't she have parents?

MRS PHILLIPS: She said. They have this market garden. You

should have said if you'd minded.

PHILLIPS: I don't mind. You'd think they'd mind: too busy with the yellow sprouting broccoli. You're the one I'd have thought would have minded.

MRS PHILLIPS: Why me? I don't mind. I think it's rather nice. I think it's rather a compliment.

PHILLIPS: Who to?

MRS PHILLIPS: To us. To the way we've brought him up. If it's not here it's somewhere else. The back of the car.

PHILLIPS: I'd never have brought anybody home. Not for the night.

MRS PHILLIPS: Your childhood was different.

PHILLIPS: Why?

MRS PHILLIPS: Well – Ireland.

In bed, a little later.

PHILLIPS: It's not in bad taste?

MRS PHILLIPS: What?

PHILLIPS: I just wondered if it was in bad taste.

(*The house is silent.*)

11. INT. PHILLIPS'S HOME: BEDROOM. DAWN

Some noise has awakened PHILLIPS. *Maybe it's a cry, but if so it's almost before the scene starts so that it may have been in his sleep or elsewhere in the house. His* WIFE *is asleep. He lies awake. Listening. He gets up and looks out into the garden. Dawn. No sound in the house.*

12. INT. PHILLIPS'S HOME: ROBIN'S BEDROOM. DAWN

From JENNIFER's *point of view, we see* PHILLIPS *in his dressing gown standing in the garden.* JENNIFER, *naked, is looking out of the window.* PHILLIPS *turns and sees her.*

JENNIFER: There's somebody in the garden.

ROBIN: (*Leaning up on one elbow and looking.*) It's only Dad.

JENNIFER: He saw me.
ROBIN: So what? Stroke my back.

13. INT. SUNLEY HOUSE: GROUND FLOOR. DAY
A group of MEN, PHILLIPS *among them, is walking towards the entrance door at the end of the ground-floor lobby. They are talking, and we hear talking but not what they are saying.*

We are seeing this from the point of view of a COMMISSIONAIRE *in British Legion uniform. He watches the party go out of the door, at which he limps over and locks the doors with a lock and chain round the handles.*

As the party drives away PHILLIPS *comes back and knocks on the glass, mouthing something we can't hear. The* COMMISSIONAIRE *laboriously unlocks the door again.*
PHILLIPS: I don't have my briefcase. I must have left it
    upstairs.
    (*He walks towards the lift.*)

14. INT. SUNLEY HOUSE: LIFT. DAY
PHILLIPS *alone in the lift.*

15. INT. SUNLEY HOUSE: UPPER FLOOR. DAY
PHILLIPS *on the upper floor where he has left his briefcase. We see for the first time the vista of the empty floor. The rows of telephones. An echo of the Puccini he was listening to at home. He is obviously taken with the place.*

16. INT. SUNLEY HOUSE: TOP FLOOR. DAY
PHILLIPS *goes through the fire exit and goes upstairs to the unfinished floor. The floor is uncarpeted and still strewn with builder's debris.* PHILLIPS *walks round it. Looks out of the window. There is a view on to the rooftop of the next building where there is a little one-storey house, palings, a pram, potted plants and washing out. A* YOUNG WOMAN *rocks the pram. A* YOUNG MAN *waters the plants.* PHILLIPS *sits down, smiling.*

17. INT. SUNLEY HOUSE: GROUND FLOOR. DAY
COMMISSIONAIRE *waiting impatiently below.* PHILLIPS *joins him and they walk across to the entrance.*
COMMISSIONAIRE: We'll go out the bottom way. That's all locked, bolted and barred.

18. INT. SUNLEY HOUSE: STAIRCASE/CORRIDOR/
COMMISSIONAIRE'S OFFICE. DAY
They are going down a blank, featureless staircase.
COMMISSIONAIRE: No nearer.
PHILLIPS: Doesn't look like it.
COMMISSIONAIRE: They'll not rent it till they get that top floor finished. It's just like the builders left it. Builders! All Micks, what do you expect? Do with a bit of life though. People coming in on a morning. Secretaries. Cleaners. Phones going. I used to be over the old Prudential building. My missis goes out cleaning. Out at five every morning, back at ten. Done a day's work before most folks have even started. Still our eldest girl's a manicurist and we've got a son in West Germany, so we haven't done too badly. That's the place by all accounts. Shops open whenever you want them. He'll shop at eleven at night sometimes. They have a different philosophy there.
PHILLIPS: (*Waiting by the door of the Commissionaire's room*) You don't live on the premises?
COMMISSIONAIRE: No fear. Hanwell. That's where I live. Why?
PHILLIPS: Nothing.
COMMISSIONAIRE: This is my little office. Or will be when you lot pull your fingers out.
PHILLIPS: Cosy.
(*The Commissionaire's office should have an armchair, table, kettle, cup. A few bare essentials.*)
We'll have the keys to this door, I suppose?

COMMISSIONAIRE: Somebody's got one. Security's got one, I know that. Coming round with that flaming dog, and many a time leaving a right parcel. I shouldn't have to have that to see to. But that's this country all over. You come through Dunkirk and end up cleaning up after a bloody Alsatian. Trade unions, no thank you.
(*He closes the door, leaving* PHILLIPS *standing outside the building.*)

19. INT. FROBISHER, RENDELL & ROSS: OUTER
OFFICE/PHILLIPS'S OFFICE. DAY

AVRIL: A negroni's nice. Gin, sweet vermouth and Campari. If anybody ever offers you one of them, say yes. I had one in Ipswich once, at the Hole in the Wall.
(CHRISTINE *is inexorably typing and does not stop throughout the scene.* RYCROFT *is sitting on her desk, using the telephone.*)

RYCROFT: What am I doing? You know me, Roger, what do you think I'm doing. I'm stretched out across the desk while Christine drops grapes into my mouth, that's what I'm doing. Just a routine Tuesday afternoon. What gives in Conveyancing? Yeah? I don't believe that for a start. Anyway, Christine's having problems with my zip so I'll tear myself reluctantly away. Yes. Don't work too hard. (*Puts the phone down.*) Who's he got seeing it today, then?

CHRISTINE: Same people who saw it last week.

RYCROFT: So they are interested?

CHRISTINE: I shouldn't think so for a minute. Difficult to adapt to their management structure is what they said. Do you know what that means? Not enough toilets. You're sitting on our *Property Gazette*.
(RYCROFT *takes it out from under him and flicks through it.*)

RYCROFT: Still, they took a second look.

CHRISTINE: What's that to you, Mr Nosey Parker? You're Residential Properties. This is Commercial. Just mind your own business.

RYCROFT: Come on, Christine.

CHRISTINE: Don't come on Christine me. My name isn't June Glazier. Besides which there's a computer programmer in Aylesbury worships the ground I walk on, so get your bum off my desk and get back where you belong. Sod it, you've made me go on treble spacing.

AVRIL: Then there's a sidecar, that's lemon juice, brandy and Cointreau. An old-fashioned: whisky, angostura and a lump of sugar. A white lady, that's white of egg, grenadine and gin. Black velvet, that's two parts of Guinness to two parts of champagne . . . I mean it's a whole world. It's my hobby really, cocktails. If I was on *Miss World*, that's what I should have to say . . .

SANDRA: What exactly is angostura?

RYCROFT: Bahrain. That's the place to be. The Persian Gulf. No fiddling about showing dismal little couples over desirable properties in Cricklewood and Tottenham, and then having to hang about while they do the ritual dance round the building societies to conjure up a mortgage. Abu Dhabi, Kuwait. That's the place to be. They don't know what a mortgage means. They fetch it in bags. Money. Not to mention s–e–x.

(*Enter* PHILLIPS *and* RYCROFT *rises unhurriedly*.)

PHILLIPS: Where?

RYCROFT: Where what?

PHILLIPS: The s–e–x.

RYCROFT: Not here.

CHRISTINE: Not for want of trying.

RYCROFT: I just popped by to say I'd got shot of Lillie Road.

PHILLIPS: Who to?

CHRISTINE: (*But still typing*) To whom.

RYCROFT: Clients. I just pushed the O.P.P. [*Outline planning permission*]

PHILLIPS: There's no planning permission on Lillie Road.

RYCROFT: It's up to them to find that out.

131

PHILLIPS: O.P.P. on Lillie Road! They'll be back.
RYCROFT: It's the old *caveat emptor*.
PHILLIPS: I'll give you 10p if they ever exchange contracts.
RYCROFT: What happened at White Elephant House?
PHILLIPS: Not keen, the clients. Not over-struck. Seemingly
    they would have to restructure.
RYCROFT: Pity.
PHILLIPS: Yes.
RYCROFT: I bet I could sell it.
PHILLIPS: I imagine you could. But would it stay sold?

20. INT. FROBISHER, RENDELL & ROSS: CORRIDOR. DAY
PHILLIPS *going along, passing* STEELE'*s office.* STEELE *and his
secretary,* MISS VENABLES, *are going through a list.*
MISS VENABLES: Ridgeway Mansions, 14 and 26.
STEELE: Ridgeway Mansions, 14 and 26.
MISS VENABLES: The Parade, Cheshunt.
STEELE: The Parade, Cheshunt.
MISS VENABLES: Harrogate, Hanaper House.
STEELE: Harrogate, Hanaper House.
MISS VENABLES: Ilkley, Moorlands Drive.
STEELE: Ilkley, Moorlands Drive.
    (*Pause.*)
MISS VENABLES: Leeds, Harehills.
STEELE: Leeds, Harehills.
MISS VENABLES: Newark, Foregate Street.
STEELE: Newark, Foregate Street.
MISS VENABLES: Bodmin, Talgarth Road.
STEELE: Bodmin, Bodmin, Bodmin. Bodmin, Talgarth Road.

21. INT. FROBISHER, RENDELL & ROSS: MISS MORPETH'S
OFFICE. DAY
PHILLIPS *is waiting by the desk of an oldish lady,* MISS
MORPETH.
MISS MORPETH: It's here somewhere.

(*She keeps pulling out keys with tattered labels.*)
Hardwick Street. No. Prestbury Road.

PHILLIPS: Prestbury Road's been sold a long time.

MISS MORPETH: Has it? Oh well. You never know when a spare
key comes in handy. Leamington Street. No. How's Mrs
Phillips? Cambridge Road. No. How's her bookbinding?

PHILLIPS: Flourishing. Flourishing.

(MISS MORPETH *opens her hand and gives him the key with a
secret smile. He takes it, also smiling as he goes.*)

MISS MORPETH: (*Calling after him*) Mr Phillips. The book.
(*Holds up an exercise book.*) Have to sign the book.
(PHILLIPS *makes a gesture to indicate he has forgotten, but it is
exaggerated, though to a very small degree, but enough to show
that it is false. He had not forgotten. He comes back and signs.*)
My system.

22. INT. FROBISHER, RENDELL & ROSS: GENTS' LOO. DAY

BLAKE *is having a pee.* BLOUNT *is inside a cubicle.*

BLAKE: Why don't we try fifty-seven?

BLOUNT: (*Out of vision*) Well, it's an interesting figure.

BLAKE: A very interesting figure. George.

(PHILLIPS *has come into the loo.*)

BLOUNT: (*Out of vision*) We might even think about fifty-eight.

BLAKE: Fifty-eight is less interesting. How's George?

PHILLIPS: Flourishing. Flourishing.

BLOUNT: (*Out of vision*) Is that George? Hello, George.

PHILLIPS: Hello, Rupert.

BLAKE: Though there is an Aga. And a walled garden.

PHILLIPS: Where?

BLOUNT: (*Out of vision*) Well, there's a garden and there's a
wall. I'm not sure there's a walled garden.

BLAKE: Cranleigh.

(BLOUNT *comes out of the cubicle.*)

Well, let's try fifty-seven then. Sevenoaks will probably
have a heart attack, but we'll cross that bridge when we

come to it. Age before beauty.
(*He lets* PHILLIPS *go out first.*)

23. INT. FROBISHER, RENDELL & ROSS: CORRIDOR/LIFT. DAY
PHILLIPS *comes out of loo followed by* BLAKE *and* BLOUNT. *He
finds* WELBY *waiting at the lift.* WELBY *immediately collars him.*

WELBY: Ah, George. I'm glad I've run across you. (*Presses
button for lift.*) I had young Rycroft in earlier on.
(PHILLIPS *doesn't help him.*)
The thing is, sometimes I wonder if we're getting a little
staid. I wonder sometimes if a little cross-fertilization
mightn't be beneficial . . . I told him.

PHILLIPS: Who?

WELBY: Rycroft.

PHILLIPS: Ah, Rycroft.

WELBY: I told him he could have a crack at our little problem
child.

PHILLIPS: Why?
(*The doors open and the lift arrives. They get in. Doors close.
Everybody facing front, looking at floor indicator.*)

WELBY: (*In slightly conspiratorial tone because overheard*) Why?

PHILLIPS: Yes.

WELBY: Seemed keen. Is keen. No harm in it. Not poaching.

PHILLIPS: Oh no.
(*Lift stops.*)

VOICE: Ten anybody?

ANOTHER VOICE: I'm ten.

VOICE: You could have fooled me.

WELBY: How's your good lady? How's the carpentry? She put
up any more shelves?

PHILLIPS: No. I think we're fairly well catered for in the shelf
department.

WELBY: She's a remarkable woman.

PHILLIPS: Yes. She's in Colchester for a few days. Looking
after her father.

WELBY: Colchester. Really. I once had a Chinese meal there.
Well, this looks very much like the ground floor. After you.

24. INT. SUNLEY HOUSE: TOP FLOOR. SUNSET
PHILLIPS *is sitting on a box in the empty room looking at it. The*
COUPLE *are outside their house. They stand by the pram and kiss.*
PHILLIPS *smiles.*

25. INT. PHILLIPS'S HOME: LOUNGE. EVENING
ROBIN *and* JENNIFER *are watching television, his arm outstretched*
behind her on the sofa. PHILLIPS *appears through the kitchen door.*
ROBIN *raises a lazy hand. Sound of television.*

26. INT. PHILLIPS'S HOME: KITCHEN. EVENING
One place laid. JENNIFER *comes through.*
JENNIFER: We had ours.
    (*She starts to get his meal out of the oven.*)
PHILLIPS: I can manage.
    (*She sits down and watches him eat without saying anything, so*
    that he has to keep looking up, giving her uneasy smiles. ROBIN
    comes through and stands in the doorway, beside her, his hand
    on her shoulder.)
ROBIN: You were late, so we had ours. You remember Jennifer.
PHILLIPS: Yes. (*Smiles.*) How was school?
ROBIN: I'm not sure. (*Asks* JENNIFER) How was school?
JENNIFER: All right. Wasn't it?
ROBIN: Yes. All right.
PHILLIPS: And what about the yellow sprouting broccoli?
    (*She smiles uncomprehendingly.* ROBIN *is suspicious he is being*
    got at.)
    In the market garden?
JENNIFER: It's more of a nursery really.

Later.
PHILLIPS *alone.*

27. INT. PHILLIPS'S HOME: LOUNGE. NIGHT
PHILLIPS *goes through into lounge.* ROBIN *and* JENNIFER *are back on the sofa. He sits apart. Watching them without them noticing.*

28. INT. PHILLIPS'S HOME: CORRIDOR. NIGHT
PHILLIPS *gets a canvas holdall.*

29. INT. PHILLIPS'S HOME: ROBIN'S BEDROOM. NIGHT
PHILLIPS *gets a bedroll from Robin's room. He looks at the room. Teddy bear, tin soldiers, stereo, pop posters, all periods of Robin's life represented in the objects there.*

30. INT. PHILLIPS'S HOME: HALL. NIGHT
PHILLIPS *holds the bag now containing the sleeping bag and waits to see if he should go into them. Decides against it. Opens the outer door quietly and goes out.*

31. INT. SUNLEY HOUSE: TOP FLOOR. NIGHT
PHILLIPS *is on the unfinished floor he looked at earlier. He is lying on the bed with his eyes open, listening to music on his cassette tape recorder.*

PART TWO

32. INT. SUNLEY HOUSE: TOP FLOOR. EARLY MORNING
PHILLIPS *puts a screen round his bedroll, etc., and leaves the building*.

33. EXT./INT. KEY SHOP. DAY
The shop advertises "Keys cut While-U-Wait".
PHILLIPS: One o'clock? It says while you wait.
WOMAN: Well, you can wait, but you don't want to be sat there all morning, do you?
PHILLIPS: What takes so long?
WOMAN: He's got arthritis.
PHILLIPS: Maybe you ought to alter the sign.
WOMAN: We're ready for retiring. We've got to come out of here anyway. All this is coming down. Is it important? The key.
PHILLIPS: It's not important.

34. INT. FROBISHER, RENDELL & ROSS: MISS MORPETH'S OFFICE. DAY
MISS MORPETH: Well, I can't find it. Mr Phillips did have it but he signed it back in first thing this morning.
RYCROFT: It can't have been lost in that short time. Are you sure he gave you it?
MISS MORPETH: He signed it in the key book. It was before I came in. (*Shows him book*.) Look. Ticked off returned.
RYCROFT: It's pathetic. A firm this size and we have a dirty little exercise book.
MISS MORPETH: We've always had an exercise book.
RYCROFT: They're coming from Croydon.
　　(*As* RYCROFT *is talking to* MISS MORPETH, WELBY *appears*,

coming into work, a wide smile as ever on his face.)

35. INT. FROBISHER, RENDELL & ROSS: OUTER
OFFICE/PHILLIPS'S OFFICE. DAY

PHILLIPS *is shaving with an electric razor.* WELBY *puts his head in.*

WELBY: Ah, George. When you've completed your *toilette*, a
   word?
   (*In the background,* AVRIL *is typing.* SANDRA *is on the
   telephone reading out details of a property.*)

SANDRA: Four bedrooms, two bathrooms, dining room, family
   sitting room, self-contained staff or granny flat. Double
   garage and two acres of paddock. And it's sixty-four.

36. INT. FROBISHER, RENDELL & ROSS: MISS MORPETH'S
OFFICE. DAY

In the background we can see MISS MORPETH *still unhappily
searching for the key.* WELBY, PHILLIPS *and* RYCROFT *talk in a
slight undertone in the foreground.*

WELBY: I think Rycroft has a point, that as a system it is lacking
   in efficiency or not so much efficiency, I think, as elegance.
   The key isn't important in itself, you say the caretaker has
   one and Security and after all nobody's going to make off
   with the building, more's the pity . . . and you did sign it
   in?
   (PHILLIPS *nods.*)
   I'm sure, yes . . . so it must be somewhere about. What is
   unfortunate is Rycroft has people coming from . . .
   Coventry?

RYCROFT: Croydon.

WELBY: Croydon. Not so far.

PHILLIPS: Croydon's not the end of the world. They can come
   another time.

WELBY: They can come another time. Still one doesn't like to
   get off on the wrong foot, particularly when Rycroft's been

so quick off the mark. Still. You're sure you returned the
. . . of course you are. Still. The other point is Miss
Morpeth, who is quite plainly not getting any younger, and
I wonder whether she might not be happier doing
something a little less demanding. What do you think?
(PHILLIPS's *face is blank.* RYCROFT *obviously agrees.*)
Peggy, perhaps you'd like to pop in and see me this
afternoon . . .
(*Another* SECRETARY *looks up, stops typing for a fraction, and
then goes on.*)
. . . if that's convenient and we'll try and sort this one out.
(*Going*) What with one thing and another this property is
turning out to be a real bugger.

37. INT. FROBISHER, RENDELL & ROSS: CORRIDOR. DAY
MISS VENABLES *is coming down the corridor with a small watering
can.*
MISS VENABLES: Morning, Mr Phillips. Morning. How's the
vine? Grapes yet? Mrs Phillips planted a vine.
PHILLIPS: Dead.
MISS VENABLES: Oh, what a shame. But be sure. Sometimes
they look dead, then suddenly they're clambering all over the
place. Now can I twist your arm? (*She has a tray of flags.*)
Kidney machines. Half an hour each day and they lead a
perfectly normal life. They're a real boon.
(PHILLIPS *forks out.* RYCROFT *is going.*)
Mr Rycroft, don't escape.
(RYCROFT *has gone.*)
Fled! Oh, he's young. They don't realize, do they?

38. FROBISHER, RENDELL & ROSS: OUTER OFFICE/
PHILLIPS'S OFFICE. DAY
PHILLIPS *goes back into his office and continues shaving.* RYCROFT
follows him. CHRISTINE *is already at her typewriter.*
PHILLIPS: Who are these Croydon people anyway?

RYCROFT: Contacts.

PHILLIPS: Sorry about that.

RYCROFT: Plenty more fish in the sea. Do you generally shave at
the office?

PHILLIPS: Sometimes.

CHRISTINE: First time I've seen it.

PHILLIPS: (*Looking out of the window*) How funny.

RYCROFT: What?

PHILLIPS: I was thinking that was a donkey. It's a chair with a
coat over it.

RYCROFT: Where?

PHILLIPS: You can't see it now.

39. INT. FROBISHER, RENDELL & ROSS: LIFT. DAY

STEELE: Reckon it's an apple and a piece of cheese today.

BLAKE: Missing the exercise?

STEELE: You know we lost the twelve thirty slot?

BLAKE: So I heard. Good old Graham.

STEELE: They were trying to sell us six o'clock.

BLAKE: Ha ha.

STEELE: I said to Graham, "Six o'clock's no good to me. Six
o'clock and I'm hopefully crawling through Totteridge."

BLAKE: Quite.

STEELE: He tends to put people's backs up.

BLAKE: He puts *my* back up. I *loved* twelve thirty.
(*Lift stops.* MARSH *gets in.*)

MARSH: Is four an improvement?

STEELE: It's an improvement, Graham, but it's not ideal.

MARSH: I know it's not ideal.

BLAKE: Twelve thirty was ideal.

STEELE: Ideal.

MARSH: Listen, Geoff. Forget twelve thirty. It was pure fluke
we ever had twelve thirty. The twelve-thirty days are over.
Twelve thirty! Everybody wants twelve thirty.

STEELE: Graham . . .

MARSH: Squash. I don't know why I ever took it on. Twelve
   thirty.
STEELE: Graham . . .
   (*The lift stops.* MARSH *gets out.*)
BLAKE: Not a happy man.
STEELE: You lunching, George?
PHILLIPS: I won't this time, Geoff.
STEELE: Hey ho.

40. EXT. KEY SHOP. DAY
Lunch hour. Busy city street. PHILLIPS *comes out of the key shop.*
Looks at watch.

41. INT. FROBISHER, RENDELL & ROSS: OUTER
OFFICE/PHILLIPS'S OFFICE. DAY
CHRISTINE *is typing.* PHILLIPS *comes in.*
CHRISTINE: Miss Morpeth's in tears in the toilet. Says she's
   going to be sacked.
PHILLIPS: She's not going to be sacked.
CHRISTINE: She says she is. She thinks it's just a preliminary to
   being computerized.
PHILLIPS: How can you computerize keys?
CHRISTINE: She says they can computerize anything these days.
   She says if they can computerize Sandra Maynard they can
   computerize her.
PHILLIPS: Sandra was estimates. That's different.
CHRISTINE: Just what I said through the door. And besides
   they didn't computerize Sandra. She just got pregnant
   about the time they were computerizing. It was sheer
   coincidence. The two weren't connected at all.
PHILLIPS: Anyway, they've found the key.
CHRISTINE: Oh, yes? Where was it? In your pocket?
PHILLIPS: Under her desk. I've spoken to Mr Welby. It's all all
   right. You'd better go get her out.
CHRISTINE: All in good time. I'm stretched across five columns

141

at the moment with a very temperamental tabulator. Do you know who I blame?

(PHILLIPS *looks out of the window*.)

PHILLIPS: Who?

CHRISTINE: Love's Young Dream. Bahrain. He's the one who wants computerizing. He was in a minute or two since. Said his people had gone off the boil and whose fault was that. They're now looking at something in Acton.

PHILLIPS: (*Looking out of the window*) It's very strange. You never think of the city as being built on land. The land underneath the city. Hills, slopes, streams. Trees. These must have been water meadows once. Cattle coming down. Reeds. And not property. *Land*.

CHRISTINE: I'll go and rescue Miss Morpeth.

42. INT. FROBISHER, RENDELL & ROSS: LADIES' LOO. DAY

AVRIL *and* LINDA *are making up, etc., in front of the mirror. One of the cubicle doors is closed.*

AVRIL: I am fed up.

LINDA: Why?

AVRIL: Had this big argument last night with Keith.

LINDA: What about?

AVRIL: Well, it started as an argument about daiquiris, then it sort of spread to the whole relationship. You see Keith was saying that a daiquiri is a short. And I said it's not a short, it's a cocktail. Cocktails aren't necessarily shorts. I mean a daiquiri's a long drink.

LINDA: What did Keith say?

AVRIL: Started on about my mother.

(CHRISTINE *comes in. Knocks on the door of the cubicle*.)

CHRISTINE: Peggy. Peggy.

MISS MORPETH: (*Out of vision*) What?

CHRISTINE: It's been found. It's all right.

(MISS MORPETH *comes out slowly*. AVRIL *and* LINDA *puzzled, watching*.)

142

43. INT. SUNLEY HOUSE: TOP FLOOR. DUSK
PHILLIPS *has brewed some coffee. He is carrying the cup and walking round the building. He sees the* COUPLE *opposite. They are sitting outside enjoying the evening. They kiss.*

44. INT. PHILLIPS'S HOME: CORRIDOR/BEDROOM. NIGHT
ROBIN *walks along the corridor dressed only in a shirt. He goes into his parents' bedroom.* JENNIFER *is already in bed. He shuts the door.*

ROBIN: I don't think it's fair.

JENNIFER: It's only so's we can sleep. Yours, it's like a doll's bed.

(ROBIN *takes off his shirt and gets into bed.*)

ROBIN: It's not fair on Mum.

JENNIFER: I dropped off in Maths this afternoon.

ROBIN: And what if he comes back?

JENNIFER: He's got a girl. Someone else.

ROBIN: Dad? Lay off. It's just not fair. I'm surprised you can't see that.

JENNIFER: Why?

ROBIN: I don't know why.

JENNIFER: Don't you like me?

ROBIN: What's that got to do with it? It's not fair on me. He should be here. Then everything would be all right. It would be good then.

JENNIFER: I like it. The place to ourselves.

ROBIN: Anyway, you should be this side.

JENNIFER: Why?

ROBIN: That's his side.

(*They slide across one another and change places.* ROBIN *is still not happy.*)

This is wrong too.

(*They change again.* JENNIFER *puts her hand on his back.*)

I don't want to do anything. Let's just sleep.

(*Pause.*)

He'll probably be here at the weekend. And after that
Mum's back.
(JENNIFER *snuggles up to him.*)
Lay off.

45. INT./EXT. SUNLEY HOUSE. DAY
Various shots of it. Streets around it empty and silent. Top floor.
Empty. The door to the roof open. Sound of church bells.

46. EXT. SUNLEY HOUSE: ROOF. DAY
A deckchair on the roof, with PHILLIPS *sitting there in the sun. A*
book. He is half-asleep. His cassette recorder playing.

47. EXT. SUNLEY HOUSE. DAY
A Securicor van draws up.

48. INT. SUNLEY HOUSE: GROUND FLOOR. DAY
SECURICOR MAN *with Alsatian dog walking across the entrance*
hall. His van visible through the window.

49. EXT. SUNLEY HOUSE: ROOF. DAY
PHILLIPS *asleep.*

50. INT. SUNLEY HOUSE: UPPER FLOOR. DAY
The SECURICOR MAN *coming through the empty floor. Past the*
lines of phones. The Alsatian sniffing the phones. The SECURICOR
MAN *goes up the stone fire staircase.*

51. EXT. SUNLEY HOUSE: ROOF. DAY
PHILLIPS *asleep on the roof. Music.*

52. INT. SUNLEY HOUSE: STAIRCASE. DAY
The SECURICOR MAN *listens. He cannot quite hear the music. The*
dog seems to hear something. The dog barks. The SECURICOR MAN
goes up the stairs. The ladder to the roof.

53. EXT. SUNLEY HOUSE: ROOF. DAY

The roof is empty. The deckchair gone. The SECURICOR MAN *locks the door.* PHILLIPS *emerges from the central-heating stack carrying his deckchair. Cautiously he looks over as far below the van drives away. Then tries door. Locked. He waits. He scouts round the roof. He finds a cradle with ropes. He starts to take the rope off. He ties the rope round a stack to secure it. Then looks over the side. Then sits down. He is terrified.*

A little later.

PHILLIPS *is still sitting there. He gets up, throws the rope with a brick on it to break the first window below the sill. The height makes him dizzy. He sits down again unable to face it. Eventually he lets himself down over the side. He clambers in at the broken window, very very frightened. Once inside some serenity returns. Which turns to pride and pleasure, as he looks down and looks up and sees what he has done.*

54. INT. SUNLEY HOUSE: TOP FLOOR. NIGHT

PHILLIPS, *very happy, goes to sleep.*

55. INT. FROBISHER, RENDELL & ROSS: OUTER OFFICE/PHILLIPS'S OFFICE. DAY

Next morning. CHRISTINE *is working at her desk.* PHILLIPS *comes briskly through the outer office*

PHILLIPS: Good morning, good morning, good morning. Morning, girls.

CHRISTINE: Good morning. Who shook your cage?

PHILLIPS: It's Monday morning, Christine. A new day. A new week. The world, Christine, is our oyster.

CHRISTINE: Mrs Phillips not back, is she?

PHILLIPS: No, Christine. Wednesday. Meanwhile we have some work to catch up with. The little matter of Sunley House. Number one on the agenda: get on to those Japs and fix up a time for tomorrow. Clear it with Mr Welby, but make it early. Nine.

CHRISTINE: Nine. Mr Welby won't like that.

PHILLIPS: Good. Number two: check with costing to see
whether they've done a breakdown on the redecorating
estimates. Three: get on to Inman and Drury. Tell them I
want the plumbing and circuit plans and I want somebody
there tomorrow morning who could do snap estimates for
possible alterations. Four: take the pillow out of the gas
oven. I shan't be needing it. And five . . .

CHRISTINE: Yes?

PHILLIPS: Not a word to our friend.

CHRISTINE: I haven't seen him this morning.

56. INT. SUNLEY HOUSE. DAY

RYCROFT *is showing round three clients. He walks ahead talking
to* ARNOLD. MILTON *and a tall, silent* AMERICAN *bring up the
rear.*

RYCROFT: We are, of course, fully air-conditioned with the
latest in underfloor central heating. The beauty of the
building is that while enjoying this splendid view . . .

ARNOLD: Kind of semi-rural, Milton.

MILTON: Grass, Arnold.

RYCROFT: . . . we are nevertheless only a few minutes from the
centre of town.

ARNOLD: That's handy. That's handy, Milton.

MILTON: It is handy.

ARNOLD: You appreciate, Mr Rycroft, that our problem is . . .
you're kind of young, aren't you, Mr Rycroft? I was just
saying to Mr Rycroft, he's kind of young, Milton.

MILTON: He is young, Arnold.

RYCROFT: We – ell . . .

ARNOLD: No, don't apologize. We like to see that . . . no, our
problem is we have a management structure which is
basically horizontal in layout. And deliberately so in order
to maximize interpersonal contact. Which rightly . . . or
possibly wrongly . . . though I happen to believe rightly

. . . is very valuable in developing a company ethic. Now this property has been custom built to house what is basically a vertical management structure. Having said that, we are at this moment in time recruiting new personnel so we are still fairly fluid in that area. But as I say that's something maybe we should want to take another look at. You don't look more than 24.

RYCROFT: That's right. Of course you appreciate we do have other clients who are very interested. A location of this sort doesn't turn up every day.

ARNOLD: *Naturellement*. When did it become available?

RYCROFT: Six months ago. Less.

ARNOLD: Funny, I had the idea it was more.

MILTON: I had the idea it was more.

ARNOLD: Still, I'm very impressed.

MILTON: I'm very impressed too.

57. INT. FROBISHER, RENDELL & ROSS: OUTER OFFICE/PHILLIPS'S OFFICE. DAY

CHRISTINE *is on the phone.*

CHRISTINE: Well, that's what Mr Phillips wants. (*Puts her hand over the phone.*) I'm not getting anywhere. Pick up two.
(PHILLIPS *picks up the phone.*)

PHILLIPS: Phillips speaking. What's the problem? Yes, well, you don't seem to be getting the message. I want a complete rundown on renovation and possible conversion costs. The details can wait but I want an outline estimate on my desk by five o'clock this afternoon. If you can't do that the contract goes to someone who can, right? I've got clients coming first thing tomorrow morning. I want to be able to quote actual facts and figures and put an estimate in their hands. Right. Right. Now you're beginning to make sense. Oh, and while we're on the subject I notice we have a broken window. You'd better get on to that.
(CHRISTINE *is lost in admiration.*)

58. INT. SUNLEY HOUSE: TOP FLOOR. DAY
They are looking at the broken window.

RYCROFT: All renovations would of course be taken up in the terms of the lease. It must have happened over the weekend.

MILTON: We're not in a violent neighbourhood here, Mr Rycroft?

RYCROFT: Not a bit.
(*They go towards the staircase.*)

ARNOLD: Curious place for a window to be broken. Hardly kids.

RYCROFT: No.

MILTON: A large bird perhaps.

ARNOLD: What about the next floor?

RYCROFT: I'm not sure . . . if you really need to see it, though of course if you want to . . .

ARNOLD: I think we do.

59. INT. SUNLEY HOUSE: STAIRCASE/TOP FLOOR. DAY

ARNOLD: I gather this top floor is unfurbished. (*Calling back down the stairs*) Milton, you appreciate this next floor is unfurbished?

MILTON: I've made a note of that, Arnold.

RYCROFT: We felt that were it to serve as an executive suite, clients would prefer a free hand with decoration and so on.

ARNOLD: (*Coming out on to the derelict floor*) Absolutely. I wonder whether . . .
(*He begins to talk in a more hushed tone to his companions, smiles apologetically at* RYCROFT, *indicating they have to have some discussion among themselves, so* RYCROFT *wanders off. He wanders round the room, eventually ending up at the screen behind which is Phillips's bedroll, etc. The other three are still talking.* RYCROFT *looks out of the window, walks along by the window and finds himself behind the screen. He takes it all in. The bed. The bible. The cassette. Cut to the other group.*)
What do you think, Milton?

MILTON: What do you think, Arnold?
(*The* THIRD MAN, *who hasn't spoken, is stony-faced.*)
ARNOLD: What do you think, Mr Alpert?
(MR ALPERT *should suddenly be revealed as the money,*
ARNOLD *and* MILTON *as minions.*)
MR ALPERT: It's shit.
ARNOLD: Mr Rycroft.
(RYCROFT *is behind the screen still. Cut to him still looking at the layout. He has found the yellow flag that Phillips bought from Miss Venables in the office.*)
RYCROFT: Coming.
(*He takes the flag, and goes over to them and they begin to walk out.*)
ARNOLD: Mr Alpert was just saying you've got a fine property here all in all, a really fine piece of real estate and in its layout and overall format somewhat reminiscent of our Brussels office . . .

60. INT. FROBISHER, RENDELL & ROSS: LIFT. DAY
PHILLIPS *leaving the building.*
PHILLIPS: (*Brightly*) Another day!
BLOUNT: For some of us. Guess where I'm headed. Harlesden. A launderette with great potential for a client with imagination.
BLAKE: Sir's just landed me with Hartlepool.
PHILLIPS: No problem there. You just plug the environment aspect. Exclusive use of local materials, all trees to remain on site . . .
BLAKE: There are no trees. There is no environment.
PHILLIPS: Well, invent one. Get the drawing office to run you up an artist's impression. Lots of elegant people sitting about the piazza in the Mediterranean-type sunshine. Better still, give it to Rycroft.
BLOUNT: I haven't seen him all day.
BLAKE: I suppose it's too much to hope he's died.

PHILLIPS: No. Probably just teething. Night all.

61. INT. SUNLEY HOUSE: TOP FLOOR. DAY
RYCROFT *waiting in Phillips's hideout.*

62. EXT. STREETS. DAY
PHILLIPS *walking through the rush-hour streets.*

63. INT. SUNLEY HOUSE: TOP FLOOR. DAY
RYCROFT *waiting.*

64. EXT. STREETS NEAR SUNLEY HOUSE. DAY
PHILLIPS *approaching the building.*

65. INT./EXT. SUNLEY HOUSE: LOBBY. DAY
PHILLIPS *comes into the building by his usual entrance, passing the Commissionaire's door when the* COMMISSIONAIRE *suddenly comes out.*

COMMISSIONAIRE: Now then. Oh. Sorry. Mr Phillips.

PHILLIPS: I was just coming in to check. I've got some clients coming tomorrow. You're here late.

COMMISSIONAIRE: I'm on watch. We're both of us on watch. Your Mr Rycroft. He's upstairs. Been there all day.

PHILLIPS: What for?

COMMISSIONAIRE: We've got a squatter. Somebody's done a squat. Here. Camp bed. Sleeping bag. One of these cassette things. The whole bag of tricks. Disgusting.

PHILLIPS: Who? How did they get in?

COMMISSIONAIRE: It's a mystery. The young fellow was trying to figure it out. Tried to put the blame on me for a start, cocky little sod. It's not my fault. He wants to surprise him. Catch him in the act. Going to stay all night if he has to.

PHILLIPS: I'd better leave him to it. Does he know who it is?

COMMISSIONAIRE: Don't know. It'll be some nasty little ginger Jesus. Smoking heroin and picking his toenails. It's not as if

it's residential accommodation. You don't squat here. You
don't squat anywhere. But you don't squat here. Anyway
(*leading the way out*) I'm off. I'm not paid for night security.
Leave him to it.
(*He locks the door.* PHILLIPS *looks at the building.*)

66. EXT. PARKLAND. DAY
We see PHILLIPS *sitting on the hill near Alexandra Palace looking
at the building. Fairly depressed.*

67. INT. FROBISHER, RENDELL & ROSS: LIFT/OUTER
OFFICE/PHILLIPS'S OFFICE. EVENING
PHILLIPS *goes back to his own office. Up in the empty lift. Through
the empty office. Covers on typewriters. Sits at his desk. Very
depressed. Thoughtful. Staring out of the window. We see him begin
to tidy his desk. Empty the drawers. Pack up. Plainly he thinks
Rycroft has found him out and he is finished.*

68. INT. SUNLEY HOUSE: TOP FLOOR. NIGHT
RYCROFT *staring out of the window of Sunley House. He sees the*
COUPLE *opposite. They are quarrelling. The young* HUSBAND *hits
his* WIFE.

69. INT. FROBISHER, RENDELL & ROSS: OUTER
OFFICE/PHILLIPS'S OFFICE. DAWN
Desk cleared. PHILLIPS *stares out of the window as dawn breaks.*

70. INT. SUNLEY HOUSE. DAY
*The sun shines on the building. Already it looks better. The party is
going round.* PHILLIPS, WELBY *and several smiling* JAPANESE.
WELBY *and* PHILLIPS *are slightly ahead,* PHILLIPS *very silent.*
WELBY: Cheer up, George. I have the impression that they're
    not displeased. They're the first clients we've had who don't
    seem worried there aren't fourteen toilets to every floor.
    (*Turns back to the leading* JAPANESE.) Of course I imagine in

Japan you daren't build anything like as substantially as this?

JAPANESE CLIENT: I'm sorry?

WELBY: (*With a pitying smile*) The earthquakes.

JAPANESE CLIENT: Oh no. Office blocks in Japan much taller than this.

WELBY: Really? Is that wise?

PHILLIPS: We don't want to show them the top floor.

WELBY: No, not if we can help it. (*Turning to the* CLIENTS) Well, that's it, gentlemen.

JAPANESE CLIENT: (*With papers*) No. No. There are nine floors. We have only seen eight floors.

(WELBY *raises his eyebrows in despair to* PHILLIPS, *but quickly turns it into another welcoming smile.*)

WELBY: Quite right. Lead the way, George. I should explain the top floor is still pretty well in a state of nature . . .

(*The* JAPANESE *follow him out, with* PHILLIPS *looking very glum and keeping in the rear.*)

71. INT. SUNLEY HOUSE: TOP FLOOR. DAY

On the top floor PHILLIPS *keeps very much in the background, watching while* WELBY *leads the* JAPANESE *round. Nearer and nearer the screen. Then away from the screen. The* JAPANESE *confer in the centre of the room. Now* WELBY *takes the* JAPANESE *on to the gallery outside the building. He describes the view.*

WELBY: I'm glad we're seeing the top floor. It gives me an opportunity to show you the executive promenade. London, gentlemen. Flower of cities all. (*Pointing out the landmarks.*) Apex House. The Vickers Building. Our old friend the Post Office Tower.

(*The* JAPANESE *have noticed* RYCROFT *asleep and are peeping through the glass at him.* PHILLIPS *looks on aghast, while* WELBY *waffles on.*)

It has been well said, gentlemen, that a man who is tired of London is tired of life.

(He suddenly realizes no one is listening, looks round, following the gaze of the astonished JAPANESE, *and sees* RYCROFT *fast asleep.)*
Good God! *(To* PHILLIPS*)* Good God!
(He rushes inside, pursued by the JAPANESE. *They all gaze at the bedroll, etc., set out behind the screen. Rycroft's trousers over a chair. As they look,* RYCROFT *sits up, unshaven.)*

WELBY: Goodness gracious me. Rycroft? Rycroft.

PHILLIPS: Rycroft?

WELBY: It's Rycroft.

(The JAPANESE *crowd round, with wondering eager smiles.)*

JAPANESE CLIENT: Lycloft? Lycloft?

RYCROFT: Sir. I've been on guard . . . I'm on the lookout . . . squatters . . .

WELBY: Lookout? Squatters?

JAPANESE CLIENT: *(Alarmed)* Squatters?

WELBY: Nonsense, gentlemen. We have no squatters. Not now, Rycroft.

RYCROFT: Sir.

WELBY: Take no notice . . . I think we've seen all this floor has to offer, gentlemen. As my colleague was saying the view is an enormous asset . . .

*(*RYCROFT *comes across the room in his shirt tails.)*

RYCROFT: Sir . . .

(The JAPANESE *laugh.)*

WELBY: Please, Rycroft. Take no notice of the young man, gentlemen . . . a precaution the insurance companies insist upon in a building of this quality. A form of residential security . . . my fault . . . I'd quite forgotten about him . . . Like Tolstoy, servants sleeping across the threshold. Do you have Tolstoy in Japan?

(He ushers them away. Behind the backs of the JAPANESE, WELBY *raises his eyebrows to* PHILLIPS *in despair as* RYCROFT *stands in the middle of the room calling after him.)*

RYCROFT: Sir . . . sir . . .

72. INT. FROBISHER, RENDELL & ROSS: OUTER
OFFICE/PHILLIPS'S OFFICE. DAY

WELBY: I could have been cross. I ought to have been cross. I
    wasn't cross since it's obviously something mental, but
    those Nips were on a knife edge. It could have gone either
    way.

PHILLIPS: He's keen. He thought he was on to something.

WELBY: A squatter, yes. I don't want to hear it, George.
    Explanations. One felt so foolish. Is he us, George? We're
    really a very old-fashioned firm. I don't think he's ever
    really appreciated that. He had poor Peggy in tears only last
    week. I don't like to see that. An employee of such long
    standing. No, I think we probably ought to let him go. For
    his own sake.

PHILLIPS: He's young. A little love nest probably.

WELBY: Don't. He was babbling on about fingerprints.
    Fingerprints. As if the police don't have enough to do. And
    did you notice, there was a *bible* there. That's always a bad
    sign. Funny, he didn't seem that type at all. Still, I think
    he'd be much happier if we were to let him go. What a
    place to choose. Such a prime location. You were quite
    right. Thought so all the time: it had to wait its turn, find
    the right client. Glad it's Japs. So reliable. Drink?

PHILLIPS: I won't.

(*They go into the corridor.*)

73. INT. FROBISHER, RENDELL & ROSS: CORRIDOR. DAY
Out of vision, we hear MISS VENABLES *and* MR STEELE *going
through their interminable list.*

MISS VENABLES: Guildford, Jenner Road.

STEELE: Guildford, Jenner Road.

MISS VENABLES: Guildford, Warren Road.

STEELE: Guildford, Warren Road.

MISS VENABLES: Earlsfield, Marsham Street.

STEELE: Earlsfield, Marsham Street.

MISS VENABLES: 16 Bradshaw Place, SE9.

STEELE: SE9, 16 Bradshaw Place.

MISS VENABLES: 12 Lord North Street, SW1.

STEELE: SW1, Lord North Street, number 12.

MISS VENABLES: 40 Smith Square, SW1.

STEELE: Smith Square, SW1, number 40.

MISS VENABLES: 14 Chelsea Square.

STEELE: 14 Chelsea Square.

(*And so on. Out of vision, we hear* BLOUNT *discussing some deal.*)

BLOUNT: Well try fifty-six. I don't hold out any hopes but try fifty-six. They're an oldish couple, he's retiring, so they are going to have to sell. Though whether they'll come down as much as that I wouldn't like to say. No. To hell with it. Try fifty-six.

(*Then, out of vision,* BLAKE *and* MARSH.)

BLAKE: So what's wrong with one thirty?

MARSH: There's a queue, that's what's wrong with it. One thirty. One thirty is as bad as twelve thirty.

BLAKE: So when are we supposed to play the bloody game: two in the morning?

MARSH: What about *before* work? Eight thirty?

BLAKE: Eight thirty! I'll be rising at dawn.

MARSH: I'll get back to you.

BLAKE: And remember twelve thirty is favourite.

74. INT. FROBISHER, RENDELL & ROSS: OUTER OFFICE/PHILLIPS'S OFFICE. DAY

The SECRETARIES *going full blast.*

AVRIL: (*While phoning*) Went out with Vince and Pauline again last night. Are you holding? They've found this pub where they do proper Manhattans. Salt round the glass, everything. Did you say three bedrooms?

SANDRA: Salt?

AVRIL: Northwood. The landlord used to work on a liner.

Three bedrooms, two reception, games room and granny
flat, is that the one? Forty-five thousand pounds.
(PHILLIPS *goes through to his office, and sits at his desk.*
CHRISTINE *is on the phone. She watches him while talking.*
His desk is still cleared, as he left it the previous night.)

CHRISTINE: Ten thousand square feet. On four floors. Yes.
Loading bay. Rear access and two minutes from the M4.
Well, that depends on the traffic, doesn't it? It says two
minutes. Right. I'll put it in the post, you'll have it in the
morning. Goodbye.
(PHILLIPS *is looking out of the window.*)

PHILLIPS: I suppose there were always buildings here. It's a
ford, you see. Where they crossed the river. There'll always
have been some kind of settlement.
(*He starts to put back his things into the drawers.*)

75. INT. PHILLIPS'S HOME: LOUNGE. NIGHT
PHILLIPS *is in the lounge listening to music.* ROBIN *is there and*
MRS PHILLIPS. ROBIN *has a new girl,* JUNE. PHILLIPS *has*
headphones on again. MRS PHILLIPS *is reading.* ROBIN *stands up*
with JUNE, *seemingly preparatory to going to bed.* PHILLIPS *takes*
off headphones.

PHILLIPS: Darling, isn't it time Robin was taking June home?
MRS PHILLIPS: Is it? I suppose it is.
ROBIN: I think she's probably going to stay.
PHILLIPS: It's after eleven. School tomorrow.
ROBIN: Why? You've let me before.
(JUNE *is in the background of this exchange but not in earshot.*)
PHILLIPS: Yes. I don't know why. But I think she probably
ought to go.
ROBIN: Dad.
PHILLIPS: No.
(*He stares the* BOY *down.*)
MRS PHILLIPS: You see, we're older than you.
(ROBIN *gives in and goes.* PHILLIPS *looks almost regretful.*)

Fascinating this book on lateral thinking.

PHILLIPS: What?

MRS PHILLIPS: I think I might try and find out more about it. Are you coming up?

PHILLIPS: In a minute.

(*She goes. He sits.*)

THE OLD CROWD

AN INTRODUCTION

Lindsay Anderson

The English are proud of their sense of humour: it is what distinguishes them from foreigners. And the mark of a sense of humour, we all know, is the ability to laugh at oneself. The English like to think they like to laugh at themselves. This may have been true once, when there was no apprehension that the Sun might one day Set. But it is not true today.

This is one truth I learned from the experience of *The Old Crowd*. Another, less disputable, is that television is the most conformist of the media, a powerful and pernicious stifler of originality, a bastion of the status quo. I am not thinking in strictly "social" terms: another connection that *The Old Crowd* made clear was that between social and artistic conformism. The almost universally apoplectic reception it received from the television critics – it was significant that the only one who understood and appreciated it was American – reminds us that the press, whether professedly Left or Right, is essentially an Establishment body. The highest ambition of a *Time Out* writer in the 1980s will be to get regular employment on *The Sunday Times* or the *Observer*. Protest is a commodity. The good ship Britannia is waterlogged in a shark-infested sea. Don't rock the boat!

Another national characteristic: the Anglo-Saxons do not favour art that claims relevance to *actuality*. By which I mean relevance to the contemporary social or political situation, whether at home or out in the world. This explains the fashionable predilection for the plays of Harold Pinter or Tom Stoppard (two authors who flatter their audiences without disturbing them), for the non-disruptive humour of *Monty Python* or *Not the Nine O'Clock News* (facetiousness masquerading as satire), for the novels of Anthony Powell or Martin Amis, the television plays of Dennis Potter. The English conception of "committed" art is *naïf*, essentially because the English intellectuals shrink from the abrasion of reality. They claim to find significance "boring" in order to disguise their fear of ideas.

These, as I say, are some ideas brought home to me by the experience of *The Old Crowd* – such a rich experience, even though it was a mere television play, written and made with a great deal of thought, fun and care. Shown once and savaged by the press with a humourless hostility as astonishing as it was suggestive. How on earth did it come to be made at all?

The responsibility must be shouldered first by Stephen Frears, and I shall always be grateful to him for it. Stephen had already directed, with great success, a number of plays written for television by Alan Bennett. When London Weekend Television invited him to make another series of six, he decided that he would direct only some of them himself. The rest he would produce. He paid me the compliment of inviting me to take one on, and sent me three scripts to choose from. I had always admired Alan's writing, for its rare combination of wit and feeling, the way it so precisely catches the poignancy as well as the comedy of existence, which we habitually express in the banal or grotesque clichés of everyday conversation. Also, sometimes hidden beneath the surface triviality of his style, I sensed strong currents of sadness and disturbance.

I liked one of these plays particularly. It happened to be the one furthest from completion. It presented the situation of a moneyed, middle-aged couple who had moved into a London house and were giving a house-warming party for a small group of their oldest and best friends. Their only problem was the loss of their furniture, misrouted on the road from Horsham and ending up in remote Carlisle. They decide to hold their party all the same, with dinner provided by caterers and served by two ambiguous waiters, who may (or may not) be out-of-work actors. As far as I remember, the piece did not have a clearly defined ending. It was called *The Old Crowd*.

This script appealed to me because it was bizarre as well as comic. Its situation struck me as more poetic than anecdotal, very apt to image certain obsessive aspects of contemporary English life: strain, menace, disintegration. And it was unfinished, which meant that there was still room in it for a director to make a creative contribution. All the same, I found that I did not call Stephen back or take the matter further. Partly this was due to an instinctive reluctance (not in the end unjustified) to enter the alien and wasteful world of television, in which one may labour long over a work that will only ever be shown once. Partly it was sheer laziness, a weariness at the thought of starting once again the long travail, the inevitable frictions and painful expense of spirit that is inseparable from any creative, collaborative undertaking. But most of all I drew back because I knew that television was traditionally and emphatically a writer's rather than a director's medium. This was a series of "Six Plays by Alan Bennett": the directors would be required simply to stage them. My formation in cinema would, I knew, impel me in quite another direction. The stage belongs to the writer and the actors: I have never cared for "director's theatre". But the cinema at its best and purest belongs to the director. Television drama is a bastard form. I could approach it only as I would approach the making of a film – personally and subjectively. And that, I felt, might well (and reasonably) be unacceptable. This was essentially why I did not call Stephen back.

He, thank goodness, called me. I told him I liked *The Old Crowd*, and that if it was a film I was being asked to undertake, I would certainly have enjoyed working on it with the author. But a collaboration for television would work only if that was truly what our relationship could be – as long, in other words, as we could both feel we were making something we could both sign. I didn't want to start anything I felt might not be harmoniously finished. And such harmony is rare.

Stephen understood what I was talking about: directors usually make the most understanding producers. He said he would talk to Alan Bennett. The next day he reported that there was no problem: Alan would be happy to collaborate. So he came round and we started work.

As is the case with every successful collaboration, it would be impossible to separate contributions: at least I could not. Alan's original script provided, of course, the starting point and the basis, the characters and the dialogue. I must take responsibility for the disruptive elements that eventually made our work so resented. I felt that I had never seen anything in television drama quite so exciting, quite so amusing or *real* as those occasional glimpses of sound equipment, even of whole camera crews that would suddenly flash before one's eyes when television plays had to be recorded "live". Without quite knowing why, I suggested we incorporate a series of such glimpses as a developing theme. The idea intrigued Alan and he agreed. Hence the repeated appearances of the camera and crew, observing the dramatic action with detached concentration, extending even to a shot in the gallery with multiple images on the monitors and Stephen Frears in the role of director, picking his shots while the Old Crowd line up to sing "Goodnight, Ladies".

"Alienation" is the Brechtian term – a translation of his *Verfremdungseffekt* – usually applied to such a style, but I have always thought this a heavy word and not a very accurate one. The real purpose of such devices, which can include songs, titles between scenes, etc., is not to *alienate* the audience from the drama, but rather to *focus* their attention on its essential – not its superficial or naturalistic – import. Of course this is almost impossible to achieve with an audience either too unsophisticated to understand the language of art, or too wedded to the aesthetic and social status quo to accept anything that hints at the subversive. For some reason, Anglo-Saxons cannot bear the idea of being taught anything: teaching implies learning, which implies development, change, growing up. Hence their violent resistance to Brecht – whom Bernard Levin once credited with the intelligence of a 6-year-old child – until his work could be safely enshrined as an elaborate but meaningless art object at the National Theatre.

Probably the most anarchic ideas in *The Old Crowd* were mine – the homage to Buñuel under the dinner table – the sexual savagery behind the television set . . . but I never felt these developments were inorganic to Alan's original conception, and nor did he. Anyway, the script as he had originally imagined it always seemed to me to carry mysterious suggestions of catastrophe and threat. Our work merely continued along these lines. We had some arguments, of course, as good collaborators must. I would object to some of the jokes with which Alan, being so good at them, would compulsively pepper his dialogue. And he would check me when my inventions became indulgent. He wanted the Lady Entertainer to sing "Pedro the Fisherman", which I thought too jokey: we settled on "Because". I wanted the Old Crowd to sing "My Old Kentucky Home"; Alan disliked the Fordian echo and specified "Goodnight, Ladies", which was, of course, the perfect choice. Fortunately both Alan and Stephen were so highly regarded by London Weekend that we were able to develop our script with complete imaginative freedom. Which is the only enjoyable way to work.

I would think that the "cinematic" as opposed to the "TV-literary" style of *The Old Crowd* would make it difficult to read. Many sequences are not dialogued at all, depending entirely on the expressiveness of the action and the performers. We were tremendously lucky in our cast. Diana Parry, the very experienced and long-suffering casting director at London Weekend, clearly thought my prejudices were as unreasonable as my ambitions were high, but by great good fortune many friends and colleagues with whom I had worked before in film and theatre were free and even eager to take part. My preference for working with actors with whom I have already collaborated happily and successfully always seems to astonish journalists. I find this strange. There is certainly nothing new about it either in theatre or film tradition. The players in *The Old Crowd* mostly knew each other and knew me from films like *This Sporting Life*, *If . . .* and *O Lucky man!* (Rachel Roberts, Peter Jeffrey, Philip Stone), as well as from the Royal Court in the great old days and, more recently, from the Lyric Theatre Company (Jill Bennett, Frank Grimes, Valentine Dyall, James Ottaway). I had known Peter Bennett ever since I'd directed him as one of the Merry Men in the classic television *Robin Hood* series; and I had known Isabel Dean so long as a friend that it felt as though we had worked together. So the Old Crowd were not strangers to me or to each other, and this helped a lot. Elspeth March as the magnificent Totty, Cathleen Nesbitt (repeatedly insisting that she had no idea what was going on, which no doubt helped her to perform with such contained acerbity), Adèle Leigh as the sweet-voiced Lady Entertainer, and David King as her accompanist – all these were cast in the usual way, from memory, suggestion and inspiration. Jenny Quayle and Martyn Jacobs, the "children", were chosen from the many talented young people whom Diana Parry produced from her long lists. Like latecomers to a party, they at first found the convivial, allusive atmosphere strange; but after three weeks' rehearsal they were each one of a seamless company.

I have emphasized the closeness and the particularity of the players in *The Old Crowd*, because I think the importance of the "chemistry" of a well-chosen cast often passes unremarked, even unperceived by critics and public alike. So how much more by the reader of a script? It is the actors, after all, who give the human feature and personality to the *idea* of the character which is all that the writer can provide. You can tell a director's personality by the actors he likes to work with – or by whether he likes to work with actors at all. (Many don't; as many don't too much care whom.) It is a human choice, not just a question of ability, nor just a question of physical rightness. What does he see in her? What does she see in him? These questions can never be answered. But they are all-important.

Nor will readers of *The Old Crowd* be able to hear the witty and emotive music written for it by George Fenton: and how can the arrival of Totty resonate fully without the broad Elgarian theme that elevates her to mythic status? They will not see the spacious and atmospheric décor provided by Jim Weatherup, nor the images lit and composed by John Fyfe and his cameramen. The script really is a blueprint, and less easy to visualize, even to the expert, than the plans for a house, an aeroplane or a food-mixer.

I used to think that I was a reasonably fast, at any rate not a wastefully slow worker; but shooting *The Old Crowd* took much longer than I anticipated. The result, unarguably, of my way of working: it certainly was not due in any way to the technicians of London Weekend. The crew operated, in fact, with extraordinary commitment – somewhat mystified, but intrigued, amused and buoyed up by a feeling that they were taking part in something extraordinary. To some extent, I'm sure, this was because I spent most of my time on the floor (cinema-style) in contact with actors and technicians, while Stephen Frears was in the control room, calling the shots. The chilling effect of reducing the director during shooting to a depersonalized voice, usually communicating with his actors only through the ear-phoned floor manager, is something I dislike intensely. I have no doubt that the sense of communal enterprise that resulted from having the director on the floor was largely responsible for the technicians' readiness to extend our last day's shooting to four o'clock in the morning. And the actors' too. Expensive, of course.

The Old Crowd took a long time to edit. There were two

reasons for this. First, a strike of production secretaries (I think) meant that nothing we shot could be "time-coded". In other words no shots could be numbered or catalogued for identification. This naturally slowed the process; but at least I could take the tapes home with me and play them until I was familiar with the coverage and the variations between takes. We spent some days in Wardour Street doing "off-line" editing. Where or how this term originates I could never discover: it meant doing a preliminary edit from a transfer of the material before making a final cut version from the original tapes. (Of course you do not "cut" tape as you do film. You transfer the exact section you want from any shot to a "master" tape, and so build up, shot by shot, your edited version. It is not easy to explain.) For some reason, also connected with the union, this process had to be kept secret. So when we finally came to edit the final version from the original tapes at London Weekend, my first edit had to be kept on a video machine in an office some distance away from the editing suite. Whenever I needed to refer to it, I had to run down the passage, hurriedly check the off-line version and then run back. Andrew Vere, who did the original cut with me, had to receive a credit as "Special Assistant to the Director". Anything more accurate, I was told, would have precipitated another strike.

This whole process took nearly a year. Not of continuous work, of course. The London Weekend editors were busy on weekly sit-coms, the sports reports and current affairs. It was not until a show date was set that I was given enough continuous time to finish the work in a few concentrated days. The technological potential of video is probably limitless; but the elaboration of equipment and the expense of using it impose huge limitations. And I shall always prefer a medium whose material I can touch, inspect against the light, run through my hand.

I was in Sri Lanka when *The Old Crowd* was shown on ITV, nearly a year after we had shot it. I was returning from a theatrical production in Australia with Rachel Roberts, and had mistaken the day of the Singapore Airlines departure for London. When I returned to my hosts, they showed me a clipping from the *Observer* which their friend Arthur C. Clarke, the famous science-fiction writer, had sent over to them. It was a review of *The Old Crowd*, as scathing as it was shallow, by their popular television critic Clive James. Its tone did not surprise me. On the cutting Arthur Clarke had written, "Poor Lindsay!" Why doesn't he write "Poor Clive James!" I wondered.

I really was not surprised. Indeed Alan Bennett recalls that I had warned him that we'd be told that I had ruined his work, and this certainly came true. But it would have been hard to anticipate the barrage of outrage that rained down on *The Old Crowd*, reminiscent of famous philistine explosions of long ago, hardly to be expected in this age of enlightenment. Indeed, speaking personally, the reception of this piece signalled the end of the acceptance which had seemed to make the sixties and early seventies at least a time of promise. The mood had changed: geniality and intelligence were out; the cat-calls came as from a single voice. "Rubbish!" (*Sunday Telegraph*). "Tosh" (*Observer*). "Meaningless" (*Sunday Express*). "Inexplicable" (*Daily Telegraph*). "Nonsensical farrago" (*Spectator*). "Raucous travesty" (*New Statesman*). The *Guardian*, the self-proclaiming defender of cultural as well as political liberality, seemed particularly incensed. Their television critic had remained comparatively calm, noting only that the piece "wasn't funny" and mourning that Alan Bennett's "absolutely unique talent" had been "crowded out". But the *Guardian*'s literary editor, Richard Gott, was so infuriated – perhaps particularly because a few days earlier his paper had devoted a whole page to a friendly account by Tom Sutcliffe of the shooting of *The Old Crowd*, that he wrote a special article, putting his feelings on record. "Miserably slender . . . insufferably pretentious . . . drivel . . . what does it all mean?" Gott's "towering rage" (his phrase) provoked a series of letters on the *Guardian*'s correspondence page that mostly echoed his indignation – "Surely an hour-long TV programme costing £250,000 cannot help in these days of pay restraint!" (K. A. Spencer, Hull) – and culminated in finely rhetorical protests from Lady Gaitskell ("Disgraceful expense . . . an intellectual and artistic 'confidence trick' . . . laced with snippets of sly, obscure pornography") and the veteran documentary director and film historian Paul Rotha ("A pretentious load of old cabbage").

Much of the criticism of *The Old Crowd* was interesting for the way it exemplified that old, unchanging philistinism which is insulted by any suggestion that an original work may deserve or require effort for appreciation, and which almost congratulates itself on its cultural ignorance. Two critics in the "quality press" imagined that the piece was derived from or influenced by Pinter: "just a protracted send-up of the works of Harold Pinter" (*Sunday Telegraph*), "full-length parody of a Harold Pinter play" (*Spectator*). The *Daily Express*, on the other hand, thought it was done "in the manner of the French cinema." *Time Out* found it "a mosaic of concerns rooted in Brecht's dramatic theory" (and failing because it was not Marxist). The *Evening News* described it as "a piece of surrealism". Richard Gott quoted a friend who thought that Frank Grimes "biting" Jill Bennett's toe was "just silly", and the *Evening News* critic asked, "What was the point of that disreputable and surly waiter getting under the table and cutting off the toes of Jill Bennett's stockings *without her objecting*?" (my italics). Really there are still a surprising number of clean-limbed English gentlemen around, who cannot tell a suck from a bite – and are charmingly perplexed when confronted by the perverse pleasures of rough trade.

Behind, or beneath this dismissive indignation, there certainly smouldered something much more interesting. A sense of affront and a defensiveness only intermittently acknowledged. The *Guardian*'s features editor (who probably thinks of himself as an anti-Establishment man) had to rationalize his bourgeois resentment with a disingenuousness typically "liberal". "Perhaps it was about the emptiness that lies at the heart of bourgeois society – in itself an excellent *though threadbare* theme." My italics again: for a theme cannot be "threadbare" and "excellent" at the same time. A *Guardian* writer who thinks that "bourgeois emptiness" is neither a valid nor a present subject must be capable of self-deception indeed. Elsewhere Gott fell back on the reactions of anonymous colleagues – "Alan Bennett's observation of middle-class manners and speech really isn't that accurate" and "Poking fun at the middle classes is not enough any more." Others were less guarded. In the *Daily Express* James Murray protested at "the brutal pillory of a class the audience were invited to despise". The *Sunday Telegraph*'s commentator on economic affairs took up the cause of the "long-suffering middle classes" and justified the status quo by quoting a new Nuffield study ("published in last week's *New Society*") which discredited the idea of a "crumbling middle class". The *Observer* critic managed another facing-both-ways jeer at Anderson's presumed conviction that "Bourgeois Society is crumbling". The determination to discredit a subversive voice was unmistakable. It was certainly significant, as I have said, that the only intelligent, restrained response to *The Old Crowd* came from the American writer Herbert Kretzmer, at that time reviewing television for the *Daily Mail*. "An unsettling production," he called it, "which said more about the state of Britain than a dozen hectoring *Panoramas*" and which "reflected, with superb skill and timing, our current mood of impotent rage and resigned despair . . . none of us, in other words, can look forward to relief and respite." Precisely (and regrettably) so.

"These days you are on your own," says Rufus grimly to George and Betty and Pauline. "Wartime." It does not seem such an extravagant comment on Britain in the eighties, in which 700 "pickets" mass daily against policemen with truncheons and riot shields to prevent one man going to work – emotion on both sides inflamed by omnipresent television cameras. . . . In which the robbing, battering and raping of old ladies as they totter home through inner-city streets, their pensions in their purses, has become commonplace. . . . In which masked sexual criminals terrorize whole counties. . . . In which ambulances fail to arrive, trains fail to run, "essential services" prove a luxury.* Our Old Crowd are keeping their eyes closed and their little flags flying in a country that presents a reality no more distorted than a cartoon by Rowlandson, a horror comic by Kafka, a satirical extravaganza by Buñuel. (I am talking of genre, of course, not of achievement.) Resolute, however, remains the resolution *not* to see, *not* to acknowledge, *not* to act. I am reminded of a notice some ten years ago of *O Lucky Man*! in the intellectual review *Encounter*, in which an academic from Oxford, John Weightman, dismissed the film because an England in which nuclear power stations exploded, policemen were corrupt and an industrial colossus was shown to be in profitable league with a reactionary African government "doesn't seem to be England at all". ("It hasn't settled for a coherent stylization . . . uninterestingly cynical.") Truly there are none so blind as those who choose not to see.

One stylistic feature of *The Old Crowd* that was not approved by Herbert Kretzmer – though it did not provoke him to the scorn and outrage of his English colleagues – was our intermittent cutaways to the studio, camera, etc. He felt that these intrusions of studio reality into the reality of the dramatic situation let the audience, so to speak, off the hook. "It's only television," they could think, and therefore evade uncomfortable implications. My own feeling is exactly the opposite. As long as the world of the drama remains an enclosed one, a self-contained fiction, the audience can regard it as "only a play". And I find the interplay or clash of "realities" stimulating rather than anodyne. Perhaps this is a matter of temperament. And anyway,

* Here Lindsay and I differ. I didn't intend *The Old Crowd* as a tract for the times, though the fact that it went out during a lorry drivers' strike led some people to think so. A.B.

one would be optimistic indeed to imagine that one could make a contemporary audience *think* with a television or any other kind of play.

Yet the English critics continue to defend the cause of naturalism with vehemence, even with fury. They dealt with the reality-juggling in *The Old Crowd* either by professing befuddlement, or by contemptuous dismissal. "Any trainee director doing that sort of thing would have been immediately sent back to training school" (*Evening News*). "Possibly a rather desperate reminder that this was a TV piece, since nearly everything – particularly acting and direction – wore a decidedly stagey air" (*Daily Telegraph*). "Stale old device . . . this tedious alienating technique . . . this drab device" (*New Statesman*).

Just why, one cannot help asking, this insistence that naturalism is the only valid style in television or cinema? Why this demand that the fiction remain enclosed, this assumption that any reminder of the author's presence is a callow solecism, "obvious", "tedious", "old hat"? (Except perhaps when excused by a foreign accent – Pirandello, Brecht, Buñuel. . . .) The *Observer* critic begged the whole question in familiar, cocksure style: "By such means a few television directors built short-lived reputations back in the fifties. Nowadays the tyro director is expected to get over that sort of thing in training school. Like good directors in any medium, the good TV directors . . . rarely draw attention to their technique." Critically this is primitive thinking: as no one should need reminding, technique and style are two different things. (The technique of *The Old Crowd* is in fact very simple.) But the prejudice behind the bluster is significant.

In an important sense, a naturalistic work accepts the world as it is. That is to say, it can criticize or expostulate only in terms of the status quo. A dissident or subversive vision demands a style that rejects the terms in which the conforming world presents itself: this is the only way it can offer a version of reality in essentially different, critical terms. The dissenting artist must hack away the props that hold up the status quo, in style as well as theme. So, if in the middle of an apparently "real" conversation between a group of confident characters the camera pans away to show *another* camera and technicians (are they technicians or are they actors?) observing them, their reality and confidence is called in question. The effect – like any sudden deflation – may also be comic.

Of course anyone watching and identifying with the characters rather than with the dissenting author will likely find this procedure disturbing. They may resent it to the point of outrage. If they are artistically *naïf*, and if it has never occurred to them that the world can be seen in any perspective other than theirs – then they may really find the whole thing "incomprehensible", "meaningless", "gratuitous". The dismissive epithets are legion. None of them, as commonly used by critics, signifies anything at all except a determination to discredit the work. And the critics who are likely to be most venomous are those who habitually pass for "satirical" or "non-conformist". The *Observer* critic, Clive James (Television Critic of the Year in 1978 and runner-up in 1979, chat-show presenter and highbrow reviewer) is a splendid representative of such licensed jesters of conformity, read because they are "amusing", not because their perceptions are either useful or correct.

To be amusing is not necessarily to be humorous. *The Old Crowd* is, of course, a comedy (however "disturbing") and, of course, there is a comic ambiguity about its stylistic departures from the norm: they are tongue-in-cheek as well as significant. I only wish that it could be seen as well as read. Perhaps one day it will be.

We almost made a film of it. In 1979 I was asked by Jorn Donner, the Finnish director then in charge of the Swedish Film Institute, to make a film for him. Neither Alan Bennett nor I felt that we had exhausted the potential of *The Old Crowd*, so I suggested a new, expanded film version. The idea was accepted. Alan and I worked on a script: we found that it would be possible to use a set already standing in the Film Institute studio: a young Polish cameraman agreed to come from Warsaw to shoot it. Then, a few weeks before we were due to shoot, the project collapsed. Donner had miscalculated his finances and neglected to secure the approval of his Board. And the unions objected.

It was a big disappointment. But of course the script is still there. And the Old Crowd are still around, or most of them. Any offers?

16 August 1984

CHARACTERS

GEORGE
BETTY
HAROLD
GLYN
PIANO TUNER
RUFUS
PAULINE
STELLA
DICKIE
OSCAR
PETER
SUE
FEMALE ENTERTAINER
MALE ENTERTAINER
TOTTY
OLD LADY

The Old Crowd was first transmitted by London Weekend Television on 27 January 1979. The cast was as follows:

GEORGE	John Moffatt
BETTY	Isabel Dean
HAROLD	Philip Stone
GLYN	Frank Grimes
PIANO TUNER	James Ottaway
RUFUS	Peter Jeffrey
PAULINE	Rachel Roberts
STELLA	Jill Bennett
DICKIE	Peter Bennett
OSCAR	Valentine Dyall
PETER	Martyn Jacobs
SUE	Jenny Quayle
FEMALE ENTERTAINER	Adèle Leigh
MALE ENTERTAINER	David King
TOTTY	Elspeth March
OLD LADY	Cathleen Nesbitt
Producer	Stephen Frears
Director	Lindsay Anderson
Designer	James Weatherup
Music	George Fenton

PART ONE

1. INT. HALL/STAIRS. NIGHT

Abstract shot of the top corner of a room near the ceiling, where walls and ceiling meet. It isn't immediately obvious where or what this shot is and over it is the sound of the single notes from a piano being tuned. A small crack appears in the wall, spreads a little, then stops. The sound of a little plaster falling.

Camera pulls back and we are in an empty London house. The house is large, roomy and built in the Edwardian period. Newly done up and decorated, but empty. The whole house should be in either white or off white, and very bright. All the lights are on. Through an open door, we see the end of a grand piano and an Alsatian dog, and the TUNER's back, or half of it.

2. INT. UPSTAIRS CORRIDOR. NIGHT

Track along an empty upstairs corridor. Similarly empty and newly decorated. The door towards the end of the corridor is open and we hear, or half hear, the murmur of conversation.

GEORGE: (*Out of vision*) Where was this?

BETTY: (*Out of vision*) This afternoon. On the phone.

GEORGE: (*Out of vision*) You've not seen her?

BETTY: (*Out of vision*) No. Not since last week. Why?

3. INT. BEDROOM. NIGHT

Camera comes through the door and we see the middle-aged couple in the process of getting changed for a dinner party. Two camp beds, sleeping bags on them, open suitcases, travelling clock. The bathroom gives off the bedroom.

GEORGE: Nothing. I just wondered what she looked like.

BETTY: Looks like? She looks what she always looks like.

> (*All the lights are on here too, with newspapers pinned across the windows.*)

179

GEORGE: She say anything else?

BETTY: Who?

GEORGE: Totty.

BETTY: No.

GEORGE: She upset?

BETTY: Not that one could tell. (*Pause.*) Then she asked me about our loose-covers. Said there was a sofa she'd been meaning to have done.

GEORGE: A sofa?

BETTY: Did I want to help choose some material? I couldn't exactly say no. Somebody's been given six months to live, you can't very well say, "Choose your own loose covers." I slightly felt she was using me. (*Goes into the bathroom.*) Anyway, I said I'd go with her. Next Tuesday.
(*She turns tap on briskly.*)

GEORGE: Poor old Totty.

4. INT. BATHROOM. NIGHT

BETTY *turns the tap off to hear him.*

BETTY: What?

GEORGE: (*Out of vision*) I said, "Poor old Totty."

BETTY: Oh. Yes.
(*She turns the tap on again, but more slowly – quickly would indicate callousness, as slowly does tact and consideration. She is looking at herself in a tiny bit of broken mirror.*)

GEORGE: (*Out of vision*) Three months puts us in Scotland.

BETTY: I don't know if I feel like Scotland this year. Do you feel like Scotland?

GEORGE: (*Out of vision*) You never feel like Scotland till it comes to the point. Our age, I suppose.

BETTY: What?

GEORGE: (*Out of vision*) Our age, I suppose. About.

BETTY: Older than us.

GEORGE: (*Out of vision*) She could have come tonight.

5. INT. BEDROOM. NIGHT

BETTY *comes out of the bathroom.*

BETTY: No.

GEORGE: No?

BETTY: It would have meant Percy.

GEORGE: Percy's in Dubai.

(*The doorbell goes. A double chime.*)

BETTY: Bell.

GEORGE: Yes.

6. INT. HALL/STAIRS. NIGHT

GEORGE *comes downstairs. He is still not completely dressed. The bell goes again. Two notes.*

7. INT. MUSIC ROOM. NIGHT

Cut to the PIANO TUNER, *who is blind. He strikes the same two notes on the piano as comprise the door chime.* GEORGE *looks in at the door as he passes. The* PIANO TUNER *turns his head slightly to indicate he knows he is there, but doesn't strike any more notes.*

8. INT. HALL/STAIRS. NIGHT

GEORGE *opens the door to* TWO MEN. *One in his fifties, the other in his twenties. Both carrying large suitcases.*

HAROLD: Mr Nelson?

GEORGE: Who are you?

HAROLD: The slaves.

GEORGE: The slaves! Of course. Enter. Enter. By all means.

(GEORGE *makes a point of closing the door, looking out first, then double locking it.*)

HAROLD: Harold.

GEORGE: Harold.

HAROLD: Glyn.

GEORGE: Glyn.

(GEORGE *has put out his hand but somehow it is not seen and he puts it away again.*)

Notice we have only the barest essentials, pending the arrival of our furniture . . . One's bits and pieces. Still I think you'll find we have gas, water and electricity. All mains services.

(*They go through the house to the kitchen at the back of the house.*)

9. INT. KITCHEN. NIGHT

There is a large crate in the middle of the empty floor.

GEORGE: They've brought your gear. Do you do this full-time?

HAROLD: We're actors. We act.

GEORGE: Acting! That is exciting. Are you "resting"?

HAROLD: Excuse me?

GEORGE: That's what it's called, isn't it, when you're out of work? Resting?

HAROLD: I call it out of work.

GEORGE: What sort of parts do you play?

HAROLD: Glyn frequently plays policeman's parts, don't you, Glyn?

(GLYN *smiles*.)

GEORGE: He's a bit slight for a policeman.

HAROLD: That's the sort of policeman he plays. The sensitive one who cracks under the strain of the constant brutality.

GEORGE: And what do you play?

GLYN: (*Unheard or whispered*) Where is the toilet?

HAROLD: I also play policemen. At a more senior level.

GEORGE: Well, it's all acting, isn't it?

GLYN: Where's the toilet?

HAROLD: Where's the toilet?

GEORGE: Are you desperate?

GLYN: I am.

GEORGE: Well, we have a slight problem. Typical story. Workmen here going on six months – floors up, ceilings down. Nightmare. Job completed. Workmen depart. We come to use the toilet and it doesn't work. Four toilets and three don't work.

HAROLD: He had every intention of going at the station only the vandals had got there first.

GEORGE: Follow me.

10. INT. HALL/STAIRS. NIGHT

They go upstairs, leaving HAROLD *alone in the kitchen.*

11. INT. KITCHEN. NIGHT

As they go upstairs cut back to HAROLD *alone in the kitchen. Having hung up his dress suit, he is brushing it down.*

12. INT. BEDROOM. NIGHT

Cut to bedroom where BETTY *is still getting ready.* GEORGE *enters, followed by* GLYN.

GEORGE: Glyn here is just going to use the bathroom.

> (GLYN *goes into the bathroom and closes the door. A wide smile from* GEORGE *to forestall criticism from his* WIFE, *who isn't pleased.*)

13. INT. HALL/STAIRS. NIGHT

GEORGE *and* BETTY *are going downstairs.*

BETTY: All I am saying is one doesn't ask to use the loo before one has barely set foot in the house.

GEORGE: They're only human.

BETTY: One leaves a decent interval.

14. INT. MUSIC ROOM. NIGHT

The TUNER *is finishing tuning the piano. As* GEORGE *and* BETTY *come in he stops and brings off a vast flourish. This pleases them. He then strikes up a rather grand waltz and as they begin to dance, we see the camera and crew in passing. During the dancing* GLYN *passes the door, or looks in but does not come in, goes away again. Suddenly the* TUNER *stops abruptly in the middle of a phrase and resumes striking his single notes.* BETTY *and* GEORGE *are brought up short and stop dancing.*

GEORGE: It's a mystery to me.

(*The* TUNER *turns his head.*)

Music.

TUNER: I came to it quite late. I used to be a policeman.

BETTY: Before you lost your sight?

TUNER: Naturally.

(*He closes the lid.*)

GEORGE: All done.

(*The* TUNER *gets up and begins to find his way about.*)

TUNER: My coat?

GEORGE: Yes. Now. Where are we? Ah, *coat.* You didn't have a stick?

(GEORGE *raises his eyes and meemoes to* BETTY *indicating "Should I tip him?" She nods confirmation.* GEORGE *takes a note out of his pocket and tries to give it to the blind man. He has some difficulty getting it into his hand.*)

TUNER: What's this?

GEORGE: It's . . . it's . . . it's just a little something.

TUNER: Is it a tip?

GEORGE: Yes. Is that all right?

TUNER: It's not enough for my fee. But as a tip it's quite generous.

GEORGE: That's what it is. The tip. Thank you.

TUNER: Thank *you.*

(*The* TUNER *has taken out his folded-up white stick, which he begins to unfold.*)

GEORGE: I say, that's handy.

(*They watch him unfold the stick in silence. The dog should also be the focus of some interest. There is a distant silence at this point to which the* BLIND MAN *and the dog hearken first, then* GEORGE *and* BETTY. *Fractional pause before the action resumes. The doorbell goes.*)

15. INT. HALL/STAIRS. NIGHT

In the hall, GLYN *is just approaching the door to answer it. He is dressed in a very ill-fitting waiter's costume, which he is still trying to adjust as he approaches the door.* GLYN *opens the door to* RUFUS *and* PAULINE, *lined up on the doorstep.* RUFUS, *a big hearty man,* PAULINE, *his assertive wife. The* BLIND MAN *moves forward with his dog.*

RUFUS: Greetings, greetings. As we enter these portals for the first time . . . greetings.

> (*The* BLIND MAN'*s way is barred.*)

GEORGE: Be right with you.

> (PAULINE *falls over the dog. She picks herself up.*)

PAULINE: What a large dog!

GEORGE: One step up. Three steps down. One. Two. Three.

> (GEORGE *doesn't go down the steps with him.*)

You'll be all right now?

> (GEORGE *closes the door –* GEORGE *makes a point of closing the door: even when* GLYN *or* HAROLD *has closed it he will make sure it actually* is *closed.*)

Sorry about that. Blind.

RUFUS: Blind? And venturing through the streets?

GEORGE: Yes. He's been a policeman.

BETTY: (*As it were beginning the ceremony of welcome afresh*) Well! You got here.

GEORGE: No problems?

> (RUFUS *takes out a large truncheon-like torch.*)

RUFUS: No problems at all.

BETTY: Oh, my goodness.

RUFUS: It's perfectly simple. You just have to walk as though you've got somewhere to go to. Somewhere you'll be missed if you don't turn up. Walk as if you meant business.

GEORGE: March.

RUFUS: Exactly.

PAULINE: But what do you do if you're a woman? What do you do if you're by yourself? Two's the minimum, *I* think.

> (GLYN *has stepped forward for their coats.*)

RUFUS: Ah. He has the look of a man wanting to take my coat.

Well, there it is. Plus the coat belonging to my good lady.

PAULINE: I'm afraid it's otter. I got it ages ago, long before there was any fuss. I don't think that matters, do you?

RUFUS: Matters to me. It's practically the only material evidence that I have spent twenty-five years up to my neck in the sewers of commerce.

(BETTY *kisses* RUFUS *and is about to kiss* PAULINE.)

PAULINE: You haven't been in contact with this virus?

BETTY: What virus?

PAULINE: Nobody knows. It's supposed to be Syrian but they're not sure. Apparently you just feel vaguely ill, slight fever, sweating. Like ordinary flu. Two hours later it's all over.

GEORGE: Better?

PAULINE: No. Dead.

BETTY: I hadn't heard about it. Had you heard about it?

(GEORGE *shakes his head*.)

PAULINE: It's everywhere. Vienna is a ghost city.

GEORGE: And are they doing anything about it?

RUFUS: What can they do about it?

PAULINE: The point is that the thing, whatever it is, thrives on antibiotics. They're its breeding ground. So of course the first places to be hit are hospitals. Don't go to hospital whatever you do.

RUFUS: Typical of this cockeyed world. The experts bring out this cure-all, before you know where you are it's killing everybody off.

BETTY: How awful.

(*The news about the virus depresses* GEORGE *and* BETTY *while cheering up* RUFUS *and* PAULINE *because they have been able to impart it.*)

PAULINE: I think germs must communicate. I think it's the only rational explanation. What a super house! (*Whirls round*.) Whee! The space! No things. No clutter. Lovely!

GEORGE: Yes, well, I ought to explain about the absence of furniture.

RUFUS: Really?

PAULINE: It's meant. Surely it's meant. Betty. Tell me
it's meant. It's the style. Simple. Scandinavian?
No?

BETTY: No. Not exactly.

GEORGE: Thing was, we'd invited everybody. Stella and Dickie,
Oscar, Peter and Sue . . .

BETTY: You and Rufus.

GEORGE: Rufus and you. Just the old crowd. Invitations all sent
out on the fairly reasonable assumption we should be pretty
well settled in by now. Horsham to here takes what? A
couple of hours?

RUFUS: At the most.

GEORGE: We know there may be extraordinary circumstances,
particularly these days, but say forty-eight hours.

RUFUS: At the outside.

GEORGE: Now ten days. Still hasn't arrived.

RUFUS: Isn't that typical?

GEORGE: And not merely is our stuff not here, it's apparently
somewhere in Carlisle.

(*During this conversation they progress into the drawing room.*)

16. INT. DRAWING ROOM. NIGHT
*There are some hired gilt chairs and a trestle table folded up against
the wall. Here too there is newspaper covering the windows. It is so
in every room.*

PAULINE: Carlisle. Oh, Betty!

(*She embraces* BETTY *in elaborate sympathy.*)

BETTY: I know!

PAULINE: I'm surprised.

RUFUS: I wish I was.

BETTY: Naturally our first thought was cancel. George was
poised at the telephone . . .

GEORGE: Then we thought no . . .

BETTY: To hell with it.

187

GEORGE: Just because some dreary little lorry driver is trying to notch up some buckshee overtime by ferrying our precious possessions to Barrow-in-Furness, why should that stop us having a nice time? Why not *camp out*?

RUFUS: Camp out?

GEORGE: *Squat*.

BETTY: So we're squatting.

GEORGE: Living out of a suitcase and loving every minute of it.

(HAROLD *approaches with a tray of drinks. Champagne, etc.*)

RUFUS: But isn't that typical? Isn't that absolutely straight down the line what we have come to expect in this God-forsaken country of ours?

(*This outburst occurs just as he is taking drinks from* HAROLD *and is directed point-blank at* HAROLD, *without being to him.*) This piss-stained ammoniacal little island. This floating urinal. Where you can't wipe your bottom without filling a form in first. And you can't transport your worldly goods from point A to point B without them getting lost in the process. Horsham to London. Two hours. Ten days. I hope you got on the phone.

GEORGE: Quite hard. The Post Office hasn't seen fit to connect us yet.

RUFUS: . . . I know, though you applied six months ago . . .

BETTY: There is a box on the corner, only . . .

RUFUS: Don't tell me.

GEORGE: . . . vandalized.

RUFUS: It's like me. Went into the office one morning. Place a shambles. Paint all over the place.

BETTY: Paint?

RUFUS: Paint, glue. Sand.

PAULINE: And that was only the half of it.

RUFUS: Soiled clothing.

BETTY: Oh, how frightful.

RUFUS: Oh, yes. It's the same everywhere.

GEORGE: It's all round here.

PAULINE: They never catch them.

RUFUS: These days you are on your own. Wartime.

    (*A pause – interrupted by the doorbell.*)

17. INT. HALL/STAIRS. NIGHT

Cut to hall as GLYN *opens the door.* STELLA *enters.* GEORGE *and*
BETTY *come to greet her, followed by* PAULINE. STELLA *is a*
stylish lady with a dull husband.

GEORGE: Stella!

BETTY: Stella! Thank God! Thank God!

STELLA: Thank God! What a trip! I'm dead. Are we late?

GEORGE: Not a bit.

STELLA: We got so lost, loster and loster. What's happened to
    the street lights?

BETTY: There were *some*.

STELLA: There aren't now. Then Dickie would insist on looking
    for a policeman.

GEORGE: A policeman!

STELLA: Of course there weren't any.

PAULINE: Stella!

STELLA: Pauline!

    (*They embrace.*)

GEORGE: Where's Dickie? Come on, Dickie, hurry up. Let's get
    the door closed.

STELLA: Dickie!

    (GLYN *has taken* STELLA's *coat. In removing it from her*
    shoulders his hand rests momentarily but purposely on her
    breast.)

    Oh, thank you very much.

18. INT. DRAWING ROOM. NIGHT

RUFUS *is left alone with* HAROLD. *We hear a reprise of the dialogue*
about the absence of furniture, such as occurred when RUFUS *and*
PAULINE *came in.*

GEORGE: (*Out of vision*) Carlisle.

STELLA: (*Out of vision*) Carlisle!

BETTY: (*Out of vision*) It was just going to be the old crowd, you
and Dickie, Rufus and Pauline . . .

GEORGE: (*Out of vision*) Oscar, Peter, Sue.

BETTY: (*Out of vision*) Thinking of course we'd be all settled in.
I mean it ought to have been here in two hours. To date it's
taken ten days.

(RUFUS *wanders round the room. Goes up to take his empty
glass to put on* HAROLD's *tray. Takes a full one. Looks at*
HAROLD *full in the face without saying anything, as the
vaguely heard dialogue continues.*)

RUFUS: I've seen you before. Haven't I?

HAROLD: (*Expressionlessly*) It's conceivable.

RUFUS: I know you. Why?

(*Enter* STELLA, *followed by* GEORGE, BETTY *and*
PAULINE.)

GEORGE: (*Finishing off his account*) . . . just because some dreary
little lorry driver is trying to notch up some buckshee
overtime.

STELLA: How exciting. How courageous. Don't you think it's
courageous? I think it's *heroic*. Rufus!

RUFUS: You're thinner.

STELLA: A bit.

PAULINE: Not anorexia?

STELLA: No. Just dry white wine.

PAULINE: I love it like this. Bare. Empty. No things. We have
too many things. We all have too many things. I feel I can
breathe here, Betty. Be . . .

RUFUS: Where's Dickie?

STELLA: Where is Dickie? I'm sure I brought him with me.

RUFUS: (*To* GLYN) You haven't put this lady's husband with the
coats, have you?

STELLA: Dickie.

DICKIE: (*Out of vision*) Coming.

(*He enters. A very mild and mousy man.*)

RUFUS: Where've you been, Dickie?
DICKIE: Valparaiso.
RUFUS: Really. Old Dickie's been in Valparaiso. Why?
STELLA: Why do you think?
PAULINE: He goes all over, don't you, Dickie?
DICKIE: Is there somewhere to sit?
GEORGE: 'Fraid not.
DICKIE: Oh. Why's that?
    (*The doorbell goes.*)

19. INT. HALL/STAIRS. NIGHT
Cut to GLYN *answering the door as the dialogue off continues as before with choruses of "Carlisle." "Carlisle?" "Carlisle." GLYN opens the door. There is nobody to be seen. He steps outside and unseen by* GLYN, OSCAR *slips behind him into the hall. He is in a broad black hat, with his coat slung over his shoulders, arms not in the sleeves.* GLYN *comes back, and is slightly startled to see* OSCAR *there already.* GEORGE *and* BETTY *come out.*
GEORGE: Oscar!
BETTY: (*Reprovingly*) Oscar!
    (OSCAR *sweeps off his hat in an extravagant gesture, then gives it, less extravagantly, to* GLYN.)

20. INT. CLOAKROOM. NIGHT
Cut to GLYN *going into the room where the coats are. He tries on the hat before setting it down beside the other coats.*

21. INT. DRAWING ROOM. NIGHT
OSCAR *is brought into the drawing room. There is less of an outburst of welcome than with the others. He goes round and kisses each of the ladies on a different part, the back of the neck, the upper arm, the neck. Very discreetly, and to nobody's surprise, except they each murmur "Oscar." He squeezes the men's hands, but doesn't shake them.*
OSCAR: And how is Stella?

STELLA: Stella is rather well. How is Oscar?

OSCAR: Oscar is all the better for seeing Stella. Pauline. (*Holds her hand.*) You are in pain.

PAULINE: No.

OSCAR: Yes. There is pain. I am never mistaken.

PAULINE: I don't think so.

OSCAR: Your back, Pauline. I feel pain in your back.

PAULINE: You're right. He's right. I am in pain. My back. I'm so used to it.

OSCAR: Let it go, Pauline. Relax. Flow. Let it go, let the pain go, flow out, down, away.

PAULINE: Oh, Oscar.

OSCAR: And what has Dickie been doing? Making lots of money in clever-Dickie fashion?

PAULINE: He made me go into commodities, didn't you, Dickie?

DICKIE: Did I?

PAULINE: Coffee. I had to buy coffee in the forward market. And a forest. We bought a forest.

BETTY: Where?

PAULINE: Where, Rufus?

RUFUS: Sussex somewhere. Someone was telling me if you'd gone into wine you couldn't lose. At the right time, of course.

PAULINE: What is the right time, Dickie?

DICKIE: Not now.

GEORGE: Somebody told me the thing to do now is sell money.

PAULINE: I hope commodities are still all right. There's nothing wrong with commodities, is there, Dickie? Should I go into money? Should I be selling money? It's all in coffee. And this forest.

DICKIE: Everybody seems to be selling money. I'm now more inclined to buy it.

PAULINE: Should I sell the forest?

DICKIE: No point in selling the forest.

RUFUS: What about the coffee?
DICKIE: It's hard to get a true picture. If we were in South
America I could tell you exactly what to do. Brazil.
Paraguay.
(*During the preceding conversation,* STELLA *promenades with*
OSCAR.)
STELLA: Paraguay! Isn't he brilliant?
(GLYN *comes round with drinks.*)
What an ill-fitting suit. (*Shrieks with laughter.*) It's bizarre.
(GLYN *says nothing.*)
RUFUS: Now, everybody. A toast. A toast to this house. To its
warmth and its welcome: the house.
GEORGE: What about a conducted tour?
PAULINE: Yes, please. I love houses.
(*They begin to troop out.*)
OSCAR: Dare one ask what it cost?
BETTY: They were asking sixty-five.
GEORGE: Sixty-eight. They started off at sixty-eight . . .
(*They go out,* GLYN *eyeing* STELLA *as they go,* STELLA *still
amused by his suit.* DICKIE *is left looking at a piece of
newspaper pinned over the window, watched impassively by*
HAROLD. *He is about to tear a piece off when* HAROLD
coughs, so therefore he writes it down.)
STELLA: (*Out of vision, calling*) Dickie.
(*He leaves, as* GLYN *begins to set up the table.*)

22. INT. HALL/STAIRS. NIGHT
*The party is trooping upstairs. There should be separate conversations
going on, parts of which we catch as they go in and out of rooms
which are chiefly along the upstairs corridor.*

23. INT. UPSTAIRS CORRIDOR. NIGHT
GEORGE: We put in an offer of fifty-six, no, fifty-four. Fifty-
four.
BETTY: Subject to contract.

PAULINE: You always have to say that. Subject to contract. Everything's always subject to contract.

GEORGE: Fifty-four was just a feeler. We never expected to get it for anything like that. Fifty-four was absurd really.

PAULINE: But that's part of the game, isn't it?

GEORGE: They then came back with sixty-four. We said fifty-six. They said sixty-two. We said fifty-eight. Then there was a terrible silence. Six weeks in which we never heard a thing. So naturally we thought, "we've lost it."

PAULINE: You weren't *gazumped*?

BETTY: I think they had someone else interested.

PAULINE: So much gazumping now, few people seem to end up in the house they first started with.

GEORGE: Anyway nine o'clock one night, I'd just got into the bath when out of the blue the telephone rings and it's their solicitor to say our offer has been accepted. So we shook hands at fifty-eight and I think we were very lucky, very lucky indeed. It would have been reasonable at sixty-eight. At fifty-eight it's a snip. The nice thing is that they got more or less what they wanted, and we got it for rather less than we'd expected so everybody's happy. That's the main thing. One doesn't like to feel one's put one over on somebody.

24. INT. DRESSING ROOM. NIGHT

BETTY: It's not a particularly safe area, of course.

RUFUS: Where is nowadays? Nowhere. Nowhere's safe. And the country's worse than the town. An elderly cousin of mine was on a bus the other day . . .

STELLA: On a bus?

RUFUS: Bus . . . nighttime, nine o'clock. Quite full, one of these jobs where the driver takes the fares.

STELLA: They're all like that now. It's the wages.

RUFUS: . . . she was on the bus opposite this young chap, 19, quite well dressed, not a *lout* anyway, sitting there *moaning*.

STELLA: Moaning?

RUFUS: Hugging himself, coat wrapped round him, rocking to
and fro, moaning. Naturally she thought drugs . . . (as one
would) . . . I say, this is a nice room . . .
(*As they pass into the next room we see the intervening wall is
plainly scenery.*)
. . . but she watched him out of the corner of her eye for a
bit and she decided, "No. This young man is ill. Really
ill." So she went and had a word with the driver. He's a bit
reluctant to stop, nine o'clock at night, middle of nowhere,
but eventually he pulls up and comes back down the bus to
investigate. And as they look at this youth they see that just
where he's hugging himself there's a great patch of blood.
Blood soaked right through his coat. (*Opening a door*)
What's in here? Ah. So the bus driver gets this young lad to
let him open his coat so they can see where he's hurt. He
opens his coat and out falls a hand. A human hand.

STELLA: His hand?

RUFUS: No, somebody else's. With a ring on it.

STELLA: What sort of ring?

RUFUS: Gold. Or something. He must have cut off the hand to
get the ring.

STELLA: And what happened then?

RUFUS: I don't know what happened then.

BETTY: And where did you say this was – New York?

RUFUS: Horsham.

25. INT. CORRIDOR. NIGHT
*They pass in and out of various rooms, appearing in the corridor from
time to time as they leave rooms and enter others.* DICKIE *is always
lagging behind.*

STELLA: I keep thinking could one go somewhere else?

GEORGE: Emigrate?

RUFUS: Why not?

BETTY: But where?

OSCAR: Quite. One almost found oneself thinking of New York.

PAULINE: *New York?*

STELLA: The thing about New York is that they will let one work.

RUFUS: Not officially. Officially one can't work. Officially one needs a green card.

GEORGE: A green card?

OSCAR: People will do anything to get a green card.

PAULINE: Does everyone have a green card?

BETTY: No. That's the point. Enormous numbers of people work in New York illegally. The Chinese. New York is full of Chinese, working, saving, going home to China, coming back. And the authorities turn a blind eye.

PAULINE: Communist China?

OSCAR: Communist China.

STELLA: How extraordinary.

BETTY: Without them the restaurant business would fall apart.

GEORGE: That couldn't happen here.

PAULINE: What?

STELLA: People working illegally.

RUFUS: Oh, no. People don't *work* here anyway, do they? Can't work legally, never mind illegally. That's the trouble.

26. INT. OLD LADY'S ROOM. NIGHT

They file into a room where an OLD LADY *is watching television. It is a programme about diseases of the eye. She is obviously enjoying it and resents being disturbed.*

GEORGE: We won't disturb you, Mother. We've given this room to Mother. It's all right . . . she's not one for social occasions. Are you, Mother?

PAULINE: It's so spacious. I long to see it furnished.

OSCAR: I imagine there'll be a good view?

GEORGE: Oh, a splendid view . . . the whole of London.

OSCAR: The whole of London? That's handy.

(*At which point we see that one of the walls is missing and there is a group of technicians watching.*)

PAULINE: You're not overlooked?

GEORGE: We have neighbours, but we've never seen them.

OSCAR: Probably foreigners. Only people who can afford to live here these days.

PAULINE: You had it rewired, of course?

GEORGE: Top to bottom.

PAULINE: It's best.

OSCAR: Cheapest in the long run.

PAULINE: Are you oil-fired?

GEORGE: Gas.

OSCAR: Safest in the long run.

PAULINE: Oh, much.

GEORGE: Thank you, Mother.

(MOTHER *gives no sign of having heard, other than wincing with irritation.*)

27. INT. DRAWING ROOM. NIGHT

GLYN *has laid the cutlery.* HAROLD *looks and sees the knives and forks are the wrong way round. He wordlessly corrects them. He looks up as* GLYN *lifts a large mirror which is on the floor by the wall to hang above the table, or prop it on the mantelpiece. As he staggers across with this mirror, helped by* HAROLD, *we see in it reflected the studio, cameras and lights. As they finish placing the mirror the doorbell goes.*

28. INT. HALL/STAIRS. NIGHT

GLYN *opens the door as* GEORGE *and* BETTY *appear at the top of the stairs at the conclusion of the tour of the house.*

BETTY: Darlings. Look who's here.

PETER: Hi.

SUE: (*Lifting her visor*) Hi. We're not late, are we?

BETTY: It's the children.

GEORGE: Not late a bit. Anyway, what's late these days?

(*They begin to take off their gear.*)

PETER: We thought we'd never make it.

PAULINE: Oh, look. It's Peter and Sue. Come on, everybody. The young people are here.

PETER: Hello, Auntie Pauline!

SUE: Hello!

PAULINE: Sue! Peter!

BETTY: We were beginning to think something had happened.

RUFUS: No fear, they can take care of themselves.

BETTY: Hugs, hugs, hugs.

PETER: Hello, Auntie Betty. Auntie Pauline. Hope we haven't held things up?

GEORGE: Not a bit. Not a bit.

(*During all this there is a lot of kissing and shaking hands.*)

PETER: How are you, sir?

RUFUS: Hello again.

PETER: Hello, sir.

RUFUS: Hello again.

PETER: Hello, sir.

STELLA: Peter, darling.

PETER: Hello, Auntie Stella. We had a couple of close shaves, but we pressed on.

GEORGE: That's the spirit.

OSCAR: Sue, my precious.

PAULINE: Let me kiss you again. Aren't you pretty? And you, dear. You're pretty too. Aren't they pretty?

GEORGE: Well. Here we all are.

(GLYN *has taken the coats and put them in the cloakroom.* HAROLD *passes through with a tray and dish cover, sidestepping the hubbub of greetings.* BETTY *now goes up to* GLYN.)

BETTY: Would you announce dinner now?

(GLYN *slouches up three steps of the staircase.*)

GLYN: (*Loudly*) Dinner is served.

(*Peal of laughter from* STELLA *as they go in.*)

29. INT. DRAWING ROOM. NIGHT
As the party comes in HAROLD *is stirring a large tureen of soup with a ladle. He finds a foreign object in the tureen and fishes it out. It is a rubber glove. He secretes it about his person but* BETTY *has seen it. She scarcely turns a hair.*

GEORGE: Right. Stella here. Pauline there. Rufus, now, don't want you sitting next to your wife, do we? You sit here. Oscar there. Peter and Sue.

STELLA: Did you do all this yourself?

BETTY: No, we've had it sent in.

STELLA: How clever. Who by?

GEORGE: This girl. She's built up a vast organization virtually from scratch and now they cater for practically everybody. The City, the Palace, government ministries. Everybody. Down to the last detail. And she started off with nothing. Now she's got an absolute fleet of vans.

RUFUS: There you are, you see. It can still be done. Provided you're prepared to work.

(BETTY *has been putting some food on a plate, while* HAROLD *waits with a tray.*)

30. INT. HALL/STAIRS. NIGHT
DICKIE *is coming down the stairs, listening to his radio. The door opens and* BETTY *comes out, followed by* HAROLD *with the loaded tray.* DICKIE *stands aside.* BETTY *and* HAROLD *go upstairs.*

31. INT. UPSTAIRS CORRIDOR. NIGHT
They go into a room. BETTY *first.*

32. INT. OLD LADY'S ROOM. NIGHT
MOTHER *is still watching television, and as avidly as before. It is a film in which some young people in a car are being pursued.*
HAROLD *brings in the tray, sets it up on the table beside her and puts it in front of her. The* OLD LADY's *attention remains primarily on the television.* BETTY *watches the film for a moment, then goes. The*

OLD LADY's *eyes glitter with pleasure and excitement as on the film the car containing the young people plunges over a cliff, dives on to some rocks and disappears into the boiling sea.*

PART TWO

33. INT. DRAWING ROOM. NIGHT
The meal is in its late stages. Pudding has been served, which most people have finished. DICKIE *is still eating.*

RUFUS: No – to tell the unpleasing truth, I don't see any light at the end of our particular tunnel. Talking to a man yesterday, managing director of a small family firm in the Midlands. Making electrical components for use in heart-support machines. Main customer, the Health Service. Employed about 250 people – mainstay of a small community. Opens his post one morning, letter from the Department of Health: "Dear Sir" and so on. New marketing developments cause cancellation of all forward orders. Components can now be obtained at a third of the price. Where? Taiwan. Come Friday night this chap locks up, puts key in an envelope, puts it through his bank manager's door. That firm is now dead. I mean, what is the point?

GEORGE: It's the same all over the country.

RUFUS: An entire community now on Social Security. Cost that in economic terms.

GEORGE: Exactly.

RUFUS: Life is poorer.

PAULINE: (*Looking at* PETER *and* SUE) Aren't they pretty? Every time I look at you I just think, "How pretty." (PETER's *mouth is full, so he doesn't speak.*)

SUE: Lovely pudding.

PAULINE: (*To* PETER) Sweet.

GEORGE: A toast. Absent friends.

ALL: Absent friends.

RUFUS: Absent friends . . . wherever they may be.

(*Pause.*)

GEORGE: Sorry. Didn't mean to put a damper on the proceedings.

PAULINE: I keep thinking about Totty.

BETTY: Yes. Poor old Totty.

OSCAR: Poor dear Totty.

PAULINE: It's not the same without Totty.

SUE: (*Who never stops smiling*) I wish I'd met her. I've heard so much about her. I thought she might be here.

STELLA: It's her blood. Something wrong with her blood.

OSCAR: Thinning.

SUE: How awful.

STELLA: How long do they think it's going to take?

OSCAR: Three months.

GEORGE: That can mean anything.

BETTY: We seem to have known Totty for ever.

OSCAR: Longer.

SUE: Does she know?

BETTY: She knows.

OSCAR: I think she's always known.

PAULINE: Peter was her special favourite, weren't you, Peter?

PETER: Well, Auntie, she is my godmother.

PAULINE: Peter's no stranger to sadness either, are you, Peter? When you've lost both your parents in two separate air crashes, you understand pain. Don't you, Peter?

PETER: I don't know, Auntie, one does one's best.

PAULINE: (*To* STELLA) He calls me Auntie, but I'm not really. He just wants someone to hold on to. I think that's why he married so young. Aren't they pretty? (*To* SUE) You're pretty too, my dear. (*To* STELLA) Isn't she?

STELLA: Yes. I gather you're also an accomplished clarinettist.

SUE: (*Smiling*) Oh, I'm not much good really.

OSCAR: Is there money? Totty.

GEORGE: I take it there is.

OSCAR: (*Talking to* DICKIE *as if to a child.*) Is there money, Dickie? Totty. Money?

DICKIE: There's some money.

RUFUS: What sort of money though? There's money and money.

BETTY: I don't think anybody's going to starve.

RUFUS: Oh, I don't think anybody's going to starve.

BETTY: Talking of starving, George, look after people.

GEORGE: More pudding, anybody? More pudding, Pauline?

PAULINE: It's delicious.

GEORGE: Stella?

STELLA: I won't, if you don't mind.

RUFUS: Have you heard about these holes?

BETTY: Holes? What holes?

RUFUS: These holes that keep appearing. There are these holes that keep appearing. Opening up in places. One in Camberwell yesterday apparently. A couple last week near Peterborough. Happening all over. Bristol. Dundee.

BETTY: How big?

RUFUS: Varies. Cardiff one was 200 feet across.

GEORGE: Cardiff? I know Cardiff.

RUFUS: Cardiff. Everywhere. Being hushed up apparently.

GEORGE: They hush everything up if they can. It must be the drought, mustn't it?

RUFUS: Or the rain. One or the other. I think there may be more to it than that.

(*During this conversation* STELLA *drops her napkin, fairly obviously, and* GLYN, *watching her, sees it fall. He gets down on the floor and there is a shot of underneath the table,* GLYN *crawling between the legs of the guests to* STELLA's *foot. He hands her up the napkin, then takes one of her shoes and puts it in his pocket. She is aware of this, but does not react. Taking a small pair of scissors from his pocket he cuts a hole in* STELLA's *stocking and sucks her big toe. The doorbell goes.*)

34. INT. HALL/STAIRS. NIGHT

HAROLD *answers the front door. A* COUPLE *stand there, muffled up. They are wearing tin hats (air-raid warden type), but the scene is in long shot so that we are not quite certain. They take them off as* HAROLD *brings them to the music room.*

35. INT. DRAWING ROOM. NIGHT

OSCAR: That's another thing they've hushed up . . . rabies in Burgess Hill.

GEORGE: Rabies in Burgess Hill? I find that hard to credit.

STELLA: Oscar, you're such a liar.

OSCAR: Four cases in the past week.

BETTY: Oh, how *depressing*.

GEORGE: No matter, life goes on.

    (HAROLD *whispers to* GEORGE.)

    Ah. We thought we'd have coffee across the hall, so if you could all bring your chairs. Follow me.

    (STELLA *follows him, still with one shoe off.*)

    Follow me, everybody.

PAULINE: (*To* PETER) I'll bring your chair, shall I?

    (*They troop out with chairs, leaving* DICKIE *to bring up the rear as usual.*)

36. INT. HALL/STAIRS. NIGHT

They cross the hall with their chairs. GEORGE *motions them to wait and he goes into the music room. Cut back to see* DICKIE *in the drawing room still eating his pudding. He switches on his radio. The group is still waiting in the hall.* GEORGE *opens the door and beckons them in.*

37. INT. MUSIC ROOM. NIGHT

The ENTERTAINERS *are standing at the piano.*

RUFUS: I say. A piano. Does this spell music? How very civilized.

SUE: (*Coming in*) Oh, how lovely! What is it? Who are they?

PAULINE: I think they must be going to perform.

(*The* ENTERTAINERS *announce a song at the piano, which is listened to in absolute poker-faced seriousness by the group.* DICKIE *as usual arrives late and doesn't bring his chair, so has to sit on one of the wide window ledges, and has his radio soon glued back to his ear. During the singing,* HAROLD *moves discreetly round the room with the silver jug of coffee, followed by* GLYN *with cream and sugar.*)

FEMALE ENTERTAINER: Good evening, ladies and gentlemen. My accompanist, Mr Gervase Howard, and I would like to give you something from our repertoire. We would like to start with one of our favourites and hope it will soon become a favourite of yours.

> Because you come to me
> With notes of love,
> And hold my hand
> And lift mine eyes above,
> A wider world of hope and joy I see
> Because you come to me.
>
> Because you speak to me
> In accents sweet,
> I find the roses waking round my feet,
> And I am led through tears and joy to thee
> Because you speak to me.
>
> Because God made thee mine
> I cherish thee
> Through light and darkness
> Through all time to thee
> And pray his love will make our love divine
> Because God made thee mine.

(*Towards the end of the song,* STELLA *gets up abruptly and leaves the room, still with one of her shoes off. Before she leaves, she gives* GLYN *her cup. He stands with the cup for a moment after she has left, then puts the cup down and follows.*)

38. INT. HALL/STAIRS. NIGHT
STELLA *goes upstairs, pauses at the turn of the stairs to look back.* GLYN *begins to mount the stairs after her. He takes out her shoe.*

39. INT. UPSTAIRS CORRIDOR. NIGHT
STELLA *goes along the corridor.* GLYN *follows her along the corridor. He stops. Drops her shoe.* STELLA *stops, comes back. Puts her foot into the shoe. She opens the nearest door and goes into it, followed by* GLYN.

40. INT. OLD LADY'S ROOM. NIGHT
It is the room where the OLD LADY *is watching television. She takes no notice. She is watching a travelogue. The fourth wall is again missing and we see camera and crew.* STELLA *draws* GLYN *to her. She takes off her ear-rings.* GLYN *puts them in his pocket.* STELLA *puts* GLYN's *fingers in her mouth, one by one. The* OLD LADY *frowns very slightly and turns the volume up.* STELLA *and* GLYN *sink down behind the television set.*

41. INT. HALL/STAIRS. NIGHT
Cut to the empty hall from the top of the stairs. The sound of applause downstairs. HAROLD *appears, leading the entertainers to the drawing room. Cries of "Bravo!"*

42. INT. MUSIC ROOM. NIGHT
GEORGE *and* BETTY *are now dancing together with* OSCAR *and* SUE. PAULINE *is dancing with* PETER. RUFUS *is settled in at the piano.* PAULINE *guides* PETER *out of the room and down the hall.*

43. INT. DRAWING ROOM. NIGHT
HAROLD *has given the two* ENTERTAINERS *something to eat and they are sitting at the dinner table, now cleared except for two plates.*

MALE ENTERTAINER: I thought that went very well. Didn't you?

FEMALE ENTERTAINER: Very well. They liked you.

MALE ENTERTAINER: They liked you too.

FEMALE ENTERTAINER: I didn't think I was quite at my best tonight.

MALE ENTERTAINER: I thought you were.

44. INT. CLOAKROOM. NIGHT
PETER *is sitting up on the mantelpiece and* PAULINE *is standing by him with her head against his knee.*

PAULINE: You see, you're so young. That's the thing about you. You're so bloody young.

PETER: Oh, I don't know.

PAULINE: Young neck. Young arms. Young legs. *Young.*

PETER: Well, I suppose I am really.

PAULINE: All you people. Young . . . *Young.* (*Lays her head against* PETER's *knee.*) We're not. We're not young. And never more shall be so. I love your young legs.

PETER: Yes, Auntie Pauline.

PAULINE: I'm not really your auntie, you know. That's just a name. (*They laugh.*)

45. INT. DRAWING ROOM. NIGHT
A party at the card table.

SUE: I think it's so sad.

BETTY: What's sad?

SUE: Your friend, Totty.

BETTY: It *is* sad. It *is* sad.

OSCAR: But one does die. That's what one does. Dies.

GEORGE: And she's had a very rich life.

OSCAR: Oh, yes.

46. INT. HALL/STAIRS. NIGHT
RUFUS *comes out, looks around, moves towards kitchen.*

He passes DICKIE.

RUFUS: Found it yet?

DICKIE: What?

RUFUS: What you're looking for.

DICKIE: It's here somewhere.

RUFUS: You'd better get a move on.

47. INT. KITCHEN. NIGHT

RUFUS *enters the kitchen where* HAROLD *is eating.*

RUFUS: Thing that I admire about you actors, thing that puzzles me, is how you remember it all.

HAROLD: Remember what?

RUFUS: Shakespeare. Those great speeches. And not only Shakespeare. The newsreaders. Never stumble, do they? Never falter. And they *care.* You can see it in their eyes. Alone in this bloody little world of ours, they *care.*

HAROLD: They're reading it. Every bloody word.

48. INT. DRAWING ROOM. NIGHT

The ENTERTAINERS *are sitting at the table eating their supper while* BETTY, GEORGE, OSCAR *and* SUE *play cards.*

BETTY: She made those holidays. The children adored her.

OSCAR: Two no trumps.

GEORGE: They were the best holidays I ever had.

OSCAR: Was that at Walberswick?

SUE: Dear old Suffolk. Oh, pass.

BETTY: I loved that house. The dogs, the children, and everybody on the veranda. Three hearts.

GEORGE: It's another world. (*Calling to the* ENTERTAINERS) All right over there?

FEMALE ENTERTAINER: Oh, yes. We're having a lovely time, aren't we?

MALE ENTERTAINER: Oh, yes.

SUE: It must have been wonderful.

(*Sound of distant howling.*)

49. INT. UPSTAIRS CORRIDOR. NIGHT
DICKIE *is wandering down the corridor, looking at various pieces of newspaper.*
DICKIE: (*Thoughtfully*) Zambia. Zambia. *Zambia.*
    (*The noise of the howling is stronger.*)

50. INT. CLOAKROOM. NIGHT
PETER *is still sitting on the mantelpiece, looking very blank.*
PAULINE *walks round him howling like a dog.*

51. INT. KITCHEN. NIGHT
HAROLD *is still eating, watched by* RUFUS. GLYN *enters and goes to the sink.* RUFUS *turns as he hears* GLYN *pissing.* GLYN *comes over to* RUFUS, *buttoning his trousers, picks up the carving knife and cuts a large slice of ham. The doorbell goes.*

52. INT. HALL/STAIRS. NIGHT
The hall is empty. The doorbell goes, unheard.

53. INT. DRAWING ROOM. NIGHT
Cut to silent shot of the bridge table. The doorbell goes.

54. INT. HALL/STAIRS. NIGHT
Loud knocking on the front door. BETTY *comes out into the hall.*
BETTY: Why doesn't somebody answer the bloody door?
    (*Guests appear from their various locations as* BETTY *opens the door. An impressive* WOMAN *is standing on the threshold.*)
    Totty! Totty!
GEORGE: Hello! Totty!
    (TOTTY *comes in, stands monumentally in the hall. She is dressed in flowing garments, rather like Dorelia John. A very "Sladey" sort of dress. She opens wide her arms.*)
TOTTY: I had to come . . . Hello everyone!
    (*There is a moment's silence then the party converges on the hall, much as they did when* PETER *and* SUE *arrived.*)

GEORGE: Look everybody! It's Totty!

(*And each person, with the exception of* DICKIE, *comes downstairs or appears saying, "It's Totty" or expressing surprise and pleasure. They come up to her and kiss her, shake her hand and she says their names, laughing and embracing.*)

RUFUS: Totty – darling!

TOTTY: Hello, my love.

STELLA: Is there one for me?

TOTTY: Dear Stella.

OSCAR: (*Kissing her hand*) Que je suis enchanté.

TOTTY: Oscar.

PAULINE: I'm so glad you came.

GEORGE: We're all glad you came.

RUFUS: Hear, hear.

PETER: Hello, Totty. Totty, you don't know my wife. Sue, Totty. Totty, Sue.

TOTTY: Dear little Peter: yesterday you were playing with your bucket and spade.

(*She embraces* SUE, *who hadn't expected to be embraced.*)

GEORGE: But ought you to be here?

TOTTY: Oh, *yes*. I can do anything. Anything I want. It's wonderful.

PAULINE: I'm glad you came.

GEORGE: We're all glad you came.

RUFUS: Hear, hear.

BETTY: Take Totty's coat, somebody.

(*She looks round for* GLYN *or* HAROLD. *They are not there.*)
George. Take Totty's coat. Come through.

TOTTY: So this is your new home?

(*They go through into the drawing room.* GEORGE *comes out of the cloakroom and follows them in. Door closed.* DICKIE *now appears, and* HAROLD *in the passage leading to the kitchen.*)

DICKIE: Did somebody come?

(HAROLD *doesn't answer.* DICKIE *opens the door and we hear* TOTTY *say "Dickie!" as the door closes again.*)

55. INT. DRAWING ROOM. NIGHT

They are all gathered round TOTTY, *who is sitting on a chair. Some are sitting at her feet, others stood behind her. Grouped.*

GEORGE: And not only is our stuff not here, it's apparently
    somewhere in Carlisle.

TOTTY: Carlisle?

STELLA: Oh don't go through all that. That's boring. What's
    been happening to you?

TOTTY: Nothing's been happening to me. I'm so happy to be
    here.
    (*She puts out her arms and takes them all in.*)
    Us.
    (GEORGE *has brought her a drink. And food. She toasts them.*)

TOTTY: (*To* GEORGE *and* BETTY) How's Giles? And Toby?

GEORGE: Toby's fine.

BETTY: And Giles is fine.

TOTTY: And Duncan and the twins?

RUFUS: They're just the same. Just the same. Alas!
    (*He laughs.*)

TOTTY: And is Donald still in Mozambique?

STELLA: Goa.

TOTTY: Isn't life strange?

GEORGE: Why?

TOTTY: Having children. Bringing them up. Sending them out.
    Wait a moment.

GEORGE: What?

TOTTY: There was something I wanted to say.

PAULINE: What?

TOTTY: No. It's gone. I was on my way here and I thought
    when I get there I'll tell them that. It'll come back.

BETTY: What sort of thing? A message?

TOTTY: Not a message, exactly.

GEORGE: Nice or nasty?

TOTTY: Oh, *nice*. Only it's gone.

GEORGE: I was just about to have a little show.

TOTTY: Oh, the old epidiascope – how splendid!

BETTY: Are you sure? Because it's your party.

TOTTY: I'd love it.

> (*The* ENTERTAINERS *are watching the group round* TOTTY. *They are still sitting at the table, and when* GEORGE *starts the slides, they turn and watch those.*)

GEORGE: Lights.

> (*Slide 1: a woman upside down.*)

Apologies.

> (*Slide 2: a prison gateway.*)

Mmm. Can't think where that one is.

> (*Slide 3: Lindsay's brother with cap; slide 4: a bandstand; slide 5: an anonymous airport.*)

Can't think why I took that.

> (*Slide 6: a meal.* PAULINE *reacts.*)

This won't mean much to you, I'm afraid.

FEMALE ENTERTAINER: Oh, no, they're fascinating, aren't they?

MALE ENTERTAINER: Yes.

> (*Slide 7: a waiter.*)

ALL: Mmmm.

> (*Slide 8: a bear.*)

PAULINE: That's Boris, dear old Boris.

> (*Slide 9: a white dog.*)

STELLA: That's Rex. Remember?

> (*Slide 10: penguins. They all laugh. Slide 11: policemen.*)

RUFUS: Who are they?

> (*Slide 12: a seashore.*)

SUE: Is that Walberswick?

BETTY: No, Tunis.

> (*Slide 13: a woman raking.*)

TOTTY: Who's that?

GEORGE: That's you, Totty.

TOTTY: Is that me? Poor me. If only I'd known.

GEORGE: Known what?

TOTTY: I don't know, just known.

(*Slide 14: two children by a pool.*)

RUFUS: That child is now in the Foreign Office.

OSCAR: She's dead.

(*Slide 15: Milos Forman.*)

STELLA: That's Percival. Before he went to India.

(*Slide 16: a cadet walking past a brass rubbing.*)

DICKIE: That boy trod on a land mine in Borneo.

(*Slide 17: a puppy in arms; slide 18: a bike.*)

GEORGE: My old Hercules.

RUFUS: And the sun went down, and the stars came out far over
the summer sea but never a moment ceased the fight of
the one and the fifty-three.

(*Slide 19: an aeroplane.*)

DICKIE: That's the Comet at Dar es Salaam.

STELLA: Up the airy mountain,
Down the rushy glen
We daren't go a-hunting
For fear of little men;

PAULINE: Wee folk, good folk
Trooping all together;
Green jacket, red cap
And white owl's feather!

(*The slides continue.*)

OSCAR: If you can talk with crowds and keep your virtue,
Or walk with kings – nor lose the common touch,
If neither foes nor loving friends can hurt you,
If all men count with you, but none too much . . .

TOTTY: No more Latin, no more Greek
No more extra work from Beak
No more beetles in my tea,
Making googly eyes at me,
No more science, no more French,
No more sitting on a hard school bench.
This time tomorrow where shall I be?

(*The final slide is of a grinning mouth with bad teeth.*)

213

PAULINE: Who's that?

GEORGE: That's Angela.

STELLA: No, it isn't. It's Hugo.

PETER: It's Auntie Clare.

BETTY: Rubbish, it's Percival. Surely it's Percival.

RUFUS: Who do you think it is, Totty?

STELLA: Totty?

PAULINE: Totty?

GEORGE: Totty. Totty. Is she asleep? (*Puts lights on.*) Totty?

OSCAR: She's dead.

STELLA: Oh, I don't think so.

OSCAR: She is dead.

GEORGE: She can't be. Totty? Totty. Totty.

BETTY: Totty.

GEORGE: Totty? Totty. Totty.

BETTY: George.

GEORGE: She's gone. She's just gone.

PAULINE: Totty? Totty.

GEORGE: No good.

OSCAR: Have we got a mirror?

> (*They lower the mantelpiece mirror and hold it with difficulty over her as* OSCAR *checks. The* ENTERTAINERS *help.*)

RUFUS: Steady, steady. Totty? Totty.

STELLA: Is she dead? What do you think, Oscar?

OSCAR: It's death all right.

PAULINE: She was having such a good time.

SUE: She doesn't look dead. I've never seen anybody dead before. Have you?

PETER: Only at school.

RUFUS: We ought to lay her out flat. Can't just have her sitting there.

OSCAR: Put her on the table.

GEORGE: That's a good idea.

RUFUS: Come on, everyone. All hands to the pumps. Prepare to lift – and lift.

(*They lift her up, like Hamlet in the final scene, and we have a top shot of* TOTTY *and her bearers, which takes in the set and the studio surroundings. The camera pans round to the gallery. From behind the director, assistants, etc., in the gallery, we see the scene in the monitors. The* FEMALE ENTERTAINER *starts to sing. The whole party joins in.*)

> Goodnight, ladies. Goodnight, ladies.
> Goodnight, ladies.
> We're going to leave you now.
> Merrily we roll along, roll along, roll along,
> Merrily we roll along,
> O'er the deep blue sea.

> Sweet dreams, ladies. Sweet dreams, ladies.
> Sweet dreams, ladies.
> We're going to leave you now.
> Merrily we roll along, roll along, roll along,
> Merrily we roll along,
> O'er the deep blue sea.

(*The* ENTERTAINERS *move to leave.*)

GEORGE: I'm so sorry.

FEMALE ENTERTAINER: It's quite all right, we understand, don't we?

MALE ENTERTAINER: Yes.

(GEORGE *gives him an envelope.*)

Goodnight.

(STELLA *indicates to* DICKIE *that they should leave.*)

GEORGE: You're not going?

STELLA: Yes, we should.

BETTY: Must you?

STELLA: Yes, we really must. Dickie.

PAULINE: We ought to.

RUFUS: Yes. I have to be up in the morning.

BETTY: You're not all going? She wouldn't have wanted you all to go.

PAULINE: She had such dignity.

RUFUS: It wasn't your fault. It wasn't anybody's fault.

GEORGE: Oh, no. It wasn't our fault. I'll have them get your coats.

SUE: Yes. You have to be up in the morning.

BETTY: Oscar, you can stay.

OSCAR: One too must go. Alas.

56. INT. HALL/STAIRS. NIGHT

The guests are standing about waiting for their coats. GEORGE *looks in the cloakroom and comes out again.* GEORGE *and* BETTY *go towards the kitchen.*

57. INT. KITCHEN. NIGHT

GEORGE *comes into the kitchen. It is empty. The large chest has gone. The door is open, no sign of anyone ever having been there.* GEORGE *is puzzled. Looks outside.* BETTY *comes in.*

GEORGE: They appear to have gone.

BETTY: Gone? Did you pay them?

GEORGE: No.

> (BETTY *picks up the carving knife.*)
> I've seen that before. They'll be back. If they haven't been paid. They'll be back.

58. INT. HALL/STAIRS. NIGHT

GEORGE *and* BETTY *come back. Only* OSCAR *is left in the hall, with* SUE *and* PETER, *getting their motor-cycle helmets on.*

BETTY: Have people gone? Where is everyone?

PETER: They went on.

OSCAR: They all went off. They wanted to stay together. I go a different way.

PETER: They said to say goodbye.

SUE: We'd better say goodbye too. Goodbye – we did enjoy it.

PETER: It was lovely seeing you all again.
GEORGE: Goodbye.
PETER: Goodbye.
BETTY: Goodbye.
SUE: Goodbye.
GEORGE: (*Seeing them through the door*) And take care.
> (GEORGE *and* BETTY *stand in the hall, the door still open.*
> GEORGE *closes the door and bolts it.*)

59. INT. DRAWING ROOM. NIGHT
GEORGE *looks in the drawing room.* TOTTY *lying on the table. He goes up to her.*
GEORGE: Totty? Totty.
> (*There is no response.*)
> I think she enjoyed it.
BETTY: Oh, yes.
OLD LADY: (*Out of vision*) George! Betty!
> (GEORGE *turns the lights off.*)

60. INT. HALL/STAIRS. NIGHT
The OLD LADY *is at the top of the stairs, walking with the aid of a Zimmer frame.*
OLD LADY: I can't get anything on my set. It's not working.

61. INT. UPSTAIRS CORRIDOR. NIGHT
They go upstairs and along the corridor. GEORGE *and* BETTY *ahead of the* OLD LADY *who comes along behind.*

62. INT. THE OLD LADY'S ROOM. NIGHT
GEORGE *stares at the set, which is showing only static. The* OLD LADY *comes in.*
GEORGE: No good. Never mind.
> (*He switches it off.*)
OLD LADY: Don't switch it off. (*Switches it on again.*) It may come on again.

(GEORGE *and* BETTY *leave the room. The* OLD LADY
continues to watch as the credits come up on the blank screen.)

CHARACTERS

FATHER
SIMON
JEREMY
MOTHER
MAITRE D'HOTEL
BERNARD
MARJORY
LEE
HARRY
JACK
MAN IN GALLERY
GALLERY ATTENDANT
MISS BECKINSALE
CUSTOMER IN SHOE SHOP
MISS BRUNSKILL
SHIRLEY
SECOND CUSTOMER IN SHOE SHOP
MR BYWATERS
IRIS BUTTERFIELD
ERNEST FLETCHER
CHRISTINE
STANLEY
MR TURNBULL
ALF
CYRIL
VIC
DUGGIE
JANE
LIZ
FIRST ORDERLY

SECOND ORDERLY
MRS BEEVERS
MR BEEVERS
OLD IRIS
STAFF NURSE
IRIS

HOTEL VISITORS and STAFF, MEN at CLUB, OAPs at CONCERT,
FACTORY WORKERS, COFFEE-SHOP CUSTOMERS,
HOSPITAL PATIENTS and STAFF, etc.

Afternoon Off was first transmitted by London Weekend Television on 3 February 1979. The cast included:

FATHER	Benjamin Whitrow
MOTHER	Angela Morant
BERNARD	Philip Jackson
MARJORY	Harold Innocent
LEE	Henry Man
HARRY	Harry Markham
JACK	Jackie Shin
MAN IN GALLERY	Stan Richards
GALLERY ATTENDANT	Peter Postlethwaite
MISS BECKINSALE	Elizabeth Spriggs
CUSTOMER IN SHOE SHOP	Carol Macready
MISS BRUNSKILL	Joan Scott
SHIRLEY	Angela Curran
MR BYWATERS	Peter Butterworth
IRIS BUTTERFIELD	Patricia Baker
ERNEST FLETCHER	Douglas Quarterman
CHRISTINE	Janine Duvitski
STANLEY	Alan Bennett
MR TURNBULL	Richard Griffiths
ALF	Paul Shane
CYRIL	Neville Smith
VIC	Bernard Wrigley
DUGGIE	John Normington
JANE	Anna Massey
LIZ	Stephanie Cole
FIRST ORDERLY	Silvia Brayshay
SECOND ORDERLY	Vicky Ireland

MRS BEEVERS	Thora Hird
MR BEEVERS	Frank Crompton
OLD IRIS	Jeanne Doree
STAFF NURSE	Lucita Lijertwood
IRIS	Sherrie Hewson
Producer and Director	Stephen Frears
Designer	Frank Nerini
Music	George Fenton

PART ONE

1. INT. HOTEL DINING ROOM. DAY

A northern spa or seaside town, Scarborough, perhaps. A large hotel dining room, empty except for a family (FATHER, MOTHER, two SONS) having a late lunch: a half-holiday from school perhaps. There is a MAITRE D'HOTEL and two waiters, BERNARD, who is local and LEE who is Cambodian or North Vietnamese. BERNARD and LEE are at a loose end, watching the diners. LEE folds napkins into cones and puts them on the tables set for the next meal. BERNARD waits to take away the dirty plates, and at the right moment LEE brings up the sweet trolley.

FATHER: Well, family! Your father begins to revive. He feels fractionally better. Now, my friend, what have you in the way of puddings to tempt my starving brood?
  (*The* MAITRE D'HOTEL *summons* LEE *with the sweet trolley.*)
  So, brats, anything there that tickles your fancy? I should tell you (*leaning in mock confidence towards the* MAITRE D'HOTEL) my children are pigs.

SIMON: Trifle.

JEREMY: Cake.

FATHER: This pig will have that and that pig will have this. Elspeth?

MOTHER: I think, perhaps, one or two figs.

FATHER: Figs for my lady wife.
  (MOTHER *nudges him.*)

MOTHER: (*Mouthing*) No cream.

FATHER: Senza crema per favore.

MAITRE D'HOTEL: And for monsieur?

FATHER: Yes. Monsieur. Monsieur will have . . . what will Monsieur have? Well, he'll have a heart attack if he has any of *that*. Ha ha. Still, it's my birthday this year, why don't I

225

treat myself? Do I spy strawberries lurking there? Strawberries it is. Splendid. Know that you have the blessings of a starving man and his offspring.

2. INT. HOTEL KITCHEN. DAY

LEE, *who has simply held the trolley impassively throughout this, now wheels it into the kitchen through some swing doors. He watches the* COOK *putting the dishes from the sweet trolley into a fridge.*

BERNARD, *the other waiter, comes in from the dining room.*

BERNARD: "Two cups of your excellent coffee and we shall have the courage to face the world." (*Addressing the swing doors*) You pillock. It's half-past bloody two. I shall be on teas in five minutes. And don't smile that inscrutable oriental smile, Genghis. This is your afternoon off. And, moreover, today is the day. Look at him, Marjory.

(MARJORY *is the nickname of the cook, a fattish man of about 50.*)

Portrait of a man about to have the best sexual experience Scarborough (*or Harrogate*) has to offer. Does it show? Is it written all over his face? Is it buggery.

(LEE *smiles.*)

That's my chicken.

MARJORY: Who's the lucky recipient?

LEE: Eilis.

BERNARD: No, bollock brain, Iris.

LEE: Eilis.

BERNARD: Skip it. I'll write it down. (*Takes the coffee tray.*) Here we are. Two cups of the life-giving liquid. I'd like to pour it very slowly up his nostrils.

(*He goes through the swing doors into the dining room.*)

MARJORY: Do you like young ladies, then?

LEE: Yes, yes. Very much.

MARJORY: I thought you people didn't mind one way or the other, Orientals. Same as you don't set much store by human life. Or is that just the Chinese? I had a friend from

Samoa once. He was very catholic. Very catholic indeed.
Ended up in the air force.

LEE: It is difficult.

MARJORY: I know some nice people.

LEE: Young ladies?

MARJORY: Not exactly. But you never know. One thing leads to
another. That's always been my philosophy.

LEE: I want to meet young ladies. English young ladies.

MARJORY: You can't expect them on a plate. You can't expect
anybody on a plate. Ladies. Anybody.

LEE: Eilis is Bernard's friend. She likes me. He showed her my
photograph.

(*He shows* MARJORY *the photograph. It is a passport photo of*
LEE, *grinning inanely.*)

MARJORY: There's a lot has to go into it in the way of
preparations. That is if you're thinking about bed. It has to
be a roundabout way of doing it. Are you thinking about
bed?

LEE: Yes. I have bought some chocolates.

MARJORY: Chocolates? Chocolates? They won't do it for
chocolates. In Berlin, in 1945, then they might have done it
for chocolates. But this isn't Berlin, 1945. This is
Scarborough, 1978. Things have changed. We're not a
conquered nation. There isn't a demoralized populace out
there. They won't do it for chocolates now. Berlin, you
could have had anybody you wanted for nothing. For
Nescafé. They'd do anything for Nescafé. Anything. And
now I've got drums of the stuff. It breaks your heart. A lot
more has to go into it nowadays. I've cooked soufflés and
they've not done it. Scampi in a hollandaise sauce.
Zabaglione. And nothing. The cocky little sods. I tell you,
you'll want more than Dairy Box.

3. INT. HOTEL DINING ROOM. DAY
LEE *goes back into the dining room.*

FATHER: (*Writing a cheque*) I think you'll find that if you present this at any branch of Lloyds Bank you will find yourself adequately recompensed.

MAITRE D'HOTEL: Sir.

FATHER: Well, family! On your feet. Thus fortified let us sally forth to see what the afternoon has in store.

(*They go beneath the smile of* LEE, *the scowl of* BERNARD, *and are followed by the* MAITRE D'HOTEL.)

4. INT. HOTEL STAIRS/CORRIDOR. DAY

LEE *going upstairs through the empty hotel. Along corridors where a* MAID *is changing dirty sheets, with more sheets on a laundry trolley outside the room, clean ones on another trolley.*

5. INT. ATTIC CORRIDORS. DAY

More stairs. Through a door marked "Private" and along, up and down attic corridors, round corners to his room.

6. INT. LEE'S BEDROOM. DAY

LEE *shaving at his little basin. Contents of his room: A map; smiling home photographs of a large family; a few battered paperbacks; a Playboy nude behind the wardrobe door, which also has a mirror so that we see it incidentally while he is dressing. A box of chocolates waiting.*

7. INT. HOTEL KITCHEN. DAY

BERNARD *is sitting in his white coat, with his feet up.*

BERNARD: Once again. Iris.

LEE: Eilis.

BERNARD: Iris.

LEE: Eilis.

BERNARD: You try, Marjory.

MARJORY: Iris.

LEE: Eilis.

MARJORY: If she was called Kevin there wouldn't be any

problem. Write him it down.

BERNARD: (*Shaking his head and writing*) What's her last name? I can't think of her last name. Anyway (*writing down her name*) she works in this shoe shop and she comes off at four.

LEE: Eilis.

BERNARD: (*To* MARJORY) It's his skin that does it. She loves olive skin. Crazy for it. Olive skin makes her go mental. Me, I'm the great white whale.

MARJORY: I like a texture to the skin, I must say.

(LEE *is going out*.)

Are you off then, Genghis?

BERNARD: Ta ra then, sugar. Give her one for Marjory and me.

(MARJORY *looks unhappy*.)

8. EXT. HOTEL STAFF ENTRANCE. DAY
LEE *goes out through the staff entrance of the hotel. Dustbins. Great zinc containers. Cardboard boxes.*

9. EXT. HOTEL FRONT ENTRANCE. DAY
Then past the front entrance to the hotel.

10. EXT. TOWN. DAY
The town is very quiet. Most of the shops are shut. It is early- closing day.

11. EXT. SHOE SHOP. DAY
LEE *tries to see in through the window, looking for Iris. He looks at a clock. Quarter-past three. He is early.*

12. EXT. STREET. DAY
LEE *stands in a deserted street. A* MAN *comes along and goes in an open doorway. Another* MAN *comes out.* LEE *watches as someone else goes in. He crosses the road.*

13. INT. MEN'S CLUB: STAIRS. DAY
LEE *going up a staircase.*

14. INT. MEN'S CLUB: LIBRARY. DAY
Two OLD MEN *playing draughts.* LEE *watches them for a while but they take no notice.*

15. INT. MEN'S CLUB: BILLIARD HALL. DAY
We see two OLD MEN *unlock a cue box, take their cues, put money in the meter to turn the lights on over one of the tables and start to play snooker.* LEE *watches them.*

HARRY: She was on at me again yesterday.

JACK: Who?

HARRY: My home help. She was proposing again. She keeps on proposing.

JACK: While she's doing your housework?

HARRY: Well, not while she's doing it. In the intervals between.

JACK: (*To the ball*) Keep floating, keep floating. Oh, lovely stuff.

HARRY: They're not supposed to do that, you know.

JACK: Propose?

HARRY: Take advantage. There was a meals-on-wheels woman had up. (*To the ball*) Kiss, you bugger, kiss. They reckon to have to maintain professional impartiality.

JACK: One off the red. One in the bed.

HARRY: "Let's get married," she keeps on saying. "Let's go to Jersey."

JACK: Jersey?

HARRY: I know. That's what I said. And she's only about 40. Little woman. Blonde hair.

JACK: Maybe you ought to be flattered. (*To the ball*) Very nice, very nice.

HARRY: If it goes on I reckon I'm going to have to contact my social worker. She was invaluable over my rates.
 (LEE *is going out.*)

JACK: Getting quite cosmopolitan round here.

HARRY: Ay. Who was he?

JACK: He looked Chinese.

(HARRY *goes and looks after him down the stairs.*)

HARRY: It's happen one of these visiting delegations. (*Coming back to the game*) We had some people round last week from Romania.

16. INT. ART GALLERY. DAY

An ATTENDANT *is sitting on a chair at the corner of an empty room. A* MAN *in a cap wanders through, obviously passing the time on. Stops to talk to the* ATTENDANT. *The* MAN *is in his sixties, the* ATTENDANT *a bit younger. The conversation is in progress when the camera catches them.*

MAN: Now then, Neville. Not busy.

ATTENDANT: Ay. Run off us feet.

MAN: I could do with your job.

ATTENDANT: It carries its own burdens. We get that much rubbish traipsing through here now I feel like a social worker. This is one of their regular ports of call, you know. Here and the social security.

(LEE *appears, walking through the gallery.*)

They don't come in for the pictures.

MAN: No?

ATTENDANT: They come in for the central heating. Genuine art lovers you can tell them a mile off. They're looking at a picture and what they're looking for are the effects of light. The brush strokes. Economy of effect. (*Watching* LEE *all the time*) But not the lot we get. Riff-raff. Rubbish. Human flotsam. The detritus of a sick society. Shove up half-a-dozen Rembrandts and they'd never come near. Turn the Dimplex up three degrees and it's packed out.

(LEE *has sat down.*)

No sitting.

(LEE *doesn't understand.*)

No sitting. Ally-up.

(LEE *doesn't understand*.)

Keep moving.

(*He motions with his fingers, and* LEE *gets up*.)

MAN: He looks like one of these overseas visitors.

ATTENDANT: They think just because the Corporation provide seats that they're to be sat on. They're not. They're Chippendale.

MAN: That's never Chippendale, is it?

ATTENDANT: School of. Anyway, they've no business sitting down.

MAN: Oh, no.

ATTENDANT: We've got an added responsibility now. These explosive devices. I search bags. I have authority to search bags. I mean him. What's he *doing*? And they have a tradition going back to the Kamikazis. No sitting. I've told you once.

MAN: You've told him twice.

ATTENDANT: I bet I know what he wants. You're not looking for the Turner?

LEE: Sorry?

ATTENDANT: No? That's what they all want to see. Anybody who has any idea. "Where's the Turner?" Flaming Turner. I can't see anything in it. Looks as if it's been left out in the rain. And we've got all sorts in here. Penny farthings. Instruments of torture. Plus the death mask of Charles Peace. Do they want to see any of that? Do they naff. We had Kenneth Clark in here once. Same old story: "Where's the Turner?" I've never seen a suit like it. Tweed! It was like silk. Then some of them come in just because we have a better class of urinal. See the Turner, use the urinal and then off. And who pays? Right. The ratepayer.

MAN: Wicked.

ATTENDANT: Art students are another bugbear. They come in here and touch. Paw the pictures. Get their noses right up to them. Do you know what does most damage to pictures?

MAN: No.

ATTENDANT: Breath. Not chemical pollution. Human breath. And which are students now? You don't know. A beard used to be a good guide. Now they've all got them.

MAN: Ay. Our Derek has.

ATTENDANT: A beard? Your Derek? Has he given up the garage?

MAN: Oh, yes. And the launderette. He's in these transverse applicators, now, the other side of Darlington.

(*And the conversation ends, trailing away as the camera follows* LEE *out*.)

17. EXT. SHOE SHOP. DAY

LEE *walks along the street. Peers into the shop again. The* MANAGERESS *sees him, and stares back. He looks at the clock. He still has twenty minutes.*

18. INT. CHURCH. DAY

LEE *wanders round. Monuments to dead worthies. The children's corner. Pictures of Jesus. All somehow meaningless to this bland oriental gaze. There is a* WOMAN *arranging flowers in the chancel. He watches her.*

MISS BECKINSALE: I hate gladioli but at least they register. Cornflowers are my favourite, but you'd need binoculars. These are so vulgar. Almost as bad as blowsy old chrysanths. Are you keen on churches?

(LEE *smiles*.)

MISS BECKINSALE: This one's very dull.

(*She goes away to do another vase somewhere else.* LEE *wanders after her*.)

Are you a stranger to these shores? Yes? I suppose you are, going by the look of you. You aren't by any chance Buddhist, are you?

LEE: No.

MISS BECKINSALE: Just a thought. Not that anybody cares a
toss these days, we're all so ecumenical. I had a great friend
who was a Buddhist. She lived in Stroud. Ploughing rather
a lonely furrow there, I always thought. The only Buddhist
in Stroud. Vegetarian too. Dear, dear, friend. Dead now.

LEE: (*Of the flowers*) They look nice.

MISS BECKINSALE: Don't they? Not that the vicar will give
them a second look. And they won't last five minutes. That
much incense flying around.
(*She gets up laboriously and carries her kneeling mat over to
another spot and a fresh vase.*)
Don't suppose it'll be long before all they have on the altar
is a couple of rubber plants. Anything to cut costs. They
come from round you, I imagine, rubber plants? (LEE
smiles.) About the most boring plant in the world, I think.
No offence.

LEE: I am a waiter.

MISS BECKINSALE: Jolly good. We also serve.

LEE: I am meeting my girlfriend.

MISS BECKINSALE: Good for you. I was going to offer you a cup
of tea, but you're spoken for. Some other time. Done my
duty by the mission field. Betty, this Buddhist I was telling
you about, and me were going on a trip to the Far East.
Just up sticks and off. Your part of the world. Palm trees,
tropical shores. She'd been a WAAF there in the war. Just
after the war, actually. I'm not that prehistoric. Going to be
the journey of a lifetime. Deck tennis, flying fish, sarongs.
Of course there were one or two things that had to be done
first. Parents to look after. House too large. Sell the house.
Mother in a home. Who's to visit. Yours truly. Never a
clean slate somehow. We still used to talk about it over the
cocoa, our trip. And then she died. Dear, dear friend.
K. L. Singapore. Hong Kong. One of those big
might-have-beens. And now it's Scarborough. Where is it
they put garlands of flowers round your neck? Hawaii, is it?

Fiji? Somewhere. Not Scarborough.

(*A clock strikes four.* LEE *hears it and begins to go.*)

If you go out be careful and close the door. The vicar's got a big thing about saving fuel . . .

19. EXT. CHURCH. DAY

LEE *running out of the church and along the street as the clock strikes four.*

20. EXT. SHOE SHOP. DAY

LEE *outside the shoe shop. It is ten-past four. No one has come out.*
LEE, *after peering in through the window, eventually goes into the shop.*

21. INT. SHOE SHOP. DAY

The manageress, MISS BRUNSKILL, *is serving a middle-aged customer.*

CUSTOMER: I've always had eights ever since I can remember.

MISS BRUNSKILL: Madam is a wide seven.

CUSTOMER: I was told I was a narrow eight.

MISS BRUNSKILL: Not by anybody with qualifications. This is a
      broad foot.

      (*She puts a shoe on it.*)

CUSTOMER: It feels a bit short.

MISS BRUNSKILL: It shouldn't. Here is madam's big toe. Acres
      of room.

      (*The* WOMAN *tries to walk on them, hobbles up and down.*
      SHIRLEY *the girl assistant, is up a ladder, putting shoes away.*
      LEE *is waiting for her at the foot of the ladder.*)

      Miss Featherstone. You have a gentleman waiting.

SHIRLEY: Can I help you?

LEE: Iris?

SHIRLEY: Sorry?

LEE: Iris. Are you Iris?

SHIRLEY: No. Shirley.

(LEE *looks doubtfully at* MISS BRUNSKILL.)

LEE: She's Iris?

SHIRLEY: No, Iris left.

MISS BRUNSKILL: The men's department is in the mezzanine, sir.

LEE: I want to see Iris. Do you know Iris?

(MISS BRUNSKILL *is about to answer when the* CUSTOMER *hobbles up.*)

CUSTOMER: Could I try an eight? I'm sure I'm not a seven. Sevens are torture.

MISS BRUNSKILL: We don't stock that model in an eight. One moment. Whom did you say you wanted?

LEE: Iris.

MISS BRUNSKILL: Shirley. Alert Mr Bywaters.

(SHIRLEY *goes unhappily downstairs.*)

If you'll take a seat, I will be with you in one moment.

(LEE *sits down.*)

I can show you something in suede.

CUSTOMER: Suede makes my feet swell.

MISS BRUNSKILL: (*Whose attention is distracted by* LEE) There are preparations for that nowadays, madam.

(*The* CUSTOMER *looks mystified.*)

Deodorants, madam.

CUSTOMER: I said "swell", not "smell".

MISS BRUNSKILL: One moment, madam.

(MISS BRUNSKILL *goes to meet* MR BYWATERS *who has come half-way up the stairs. He waits there surveying* LEE. *Behind* LEE MISS BRUNSKILL *indicates that* LEE *is the person in question.* SHIRLEY *comes back up the stairs into the shop and looks sympathetically at him, before going on with her own work.*)

MR BYWATERS: Is this the person, Miss Brunskill?

(MISS BRUNSKILL *nods.*)

I understand you're looking for Miss Butterworth.

LEE: Iris.

MR BYWATERS: She is no longer in our employ.

LEE: Not here?

MR BYWATERS: I'm afraid not. We were forced to release her.

LEE: Where is she?

MR BYWATERS: Perhaps you could tell me? Miss Butterworth left taking with her some of our stock, namely one pair of thigh-length boots in crushed mimosa and fourteen packets of fully fashioned hosiery. The matter is now in the hands of the police. Do you know her? Is she a friend of yours?

LEE: No.

MR BYWATERS: You don't know her. Yet you are making enquiries as to her whereabouts?

LEE: No.

MR BYWATERS: No? Yes. She was a dishonest employee. I hope you're not on the same game. One of these foreign visitors who come over here for the express purpose of shoplifting, perhaps. Well, not here, young man. See that? That's a television camera. Every move you make is monitored. So don't come that game with me. If you have no intention of making a purchase I suggest you leave these premises forthwith. (LEE *goes.*) Where is Iris, indeed. I wish I knew. I say I wish I knew.

(MISS BRUNSKILL *turns back to find that her* CUSTOMER *has sneaked out after* LEE.)

22. EXT. SHOE SHOP. DAY

Outside the shop. It is raining, so the CUSTOMER *and* LEE *shelter in the doorway.*

CUSTOMER: The blighters! They always want to rule you, shops. Wide seven! I'm a narrow eight. I have been ever since I got married. Well, I'm 57 and the beggars aren't going to rule me. I'm old enough to rule myself. Then saying they smelt. They never do. Only they would if I had to cram them into a seven. Preparations. I'd look well starting on that game my age.

LEE *watches her go, but still waits, uncertain what to do. While he is waiting* SHIRLEY, *the young assistant, comes out with a* SECOND CUSTOMER *who wants to point out a pair of shoes in the window.*)

SECOND CUSTOMER: I think them's the ones I mean.

SHIRLEY: Do you still want Iris?

LEE: Iris? Yes.

SHIRLEY: I think her Dad works at Batty's. (*Gives him a piece of paper.*) Which?

SECOND CUSTOMER: Them.

SHIRLEY: Batty's.

SECOND CUSTOMER: Who wants Batty's? You want Batty's? It's at the bottom of Dickinson Road.

(*The* SECOND CUSTOMER *takes* LEE *out and points out the way. No sound.* SHIRLEY *watches as he goes and he smiles at her. We know that even though her name isn't Iris, she would have been quite prepared to fill the bill.*)

23. EXT. CHURCH HALL. DAY

LEE *is waiting at a bus stop outside the church hall. Behind him is a large noticeboard, with a hand-painted poster advertising a pensioners' concert*:

Ladies Bright Hour
Songs at the Piano
by
Iris Butterfield and Ernest Fletcher
At the Piano: Miss Tattersall
All Welcome

The sound of distant music from the hall attracts LEE's *attention. He looks at the poster. At the note in his hand. At the name "Iris".*

24. INT. CHURCH HALL. DAY

An audience of OAPs. The two SINGERS *are giving their rendition of "Pedro the Fisherman". Periodically the* OLD LADIES *join in*

and whistle the refrain. The scene is intercut with shots of LEE
*coming up the stairs backstage and eventually finding his way into
the wings.*

Pedro the fisherman was always whistling,
Such a merry call;
Girls who were passing by would hear him whistling,
By the harbour wall.
But our sweet Teresa who loved him true always knew
That his song belonged to her alone.
So they wandered hand in hand; you in love will
    understand
Why it was he whistled all the day.
And in the evening when the lights were gleaming
And they had to part,
As he sailed his boat away,
Echoing across the bay,
Came the tune that lingered in her heart.

But Pedro found the sea was drear and chose another
    course
He sold his boat and fishing gear and bought himself a
    horse.
He rode away to find the gold the sea could never bring,
To buy a dress, a cuckoo clock, a saucepan and a ring.
One day her father said to her, "Oh dearest daughter
    mine
You'll never make a lot from fish, you make much more
    from wine.
Though Miguel is rather fat, his vineyard's doing well.
So marry him and let your dreams of Pedro go to hell."

The organ peals
The choirboys sing
The priest is ready with the book and ring.

So small and white
Here comes the bride
And stands by swarthy Miguel's side.
"Will you have this man to be your lawful wedded spouse
    eternally?"
And suddenly the church is still.
They wait to hear her say, "I will",
When through the open doorway a far-off sound disturbs
    the air . . .
(*The audience begin to whistle*).

IRIS *has sent her partner,* MR FLETCHER, *offstage and now beckons him on as the returning Pedro. Thinking she is welcoming him,* LEE *ventures hesitantly on to the stage.* IRIS *who is plainly not the Iris, is mystified. The* OLD LADIES, *thinking it all part of the show, are delighted and burst out clapping.* LEE *stands on stage very puzzled.*)

PART TWO

25. INT. GENERAL OFFICE. DAY

Reception cum general office of a factory. A MAN *and a* WOMAN *in the office,* LEE *sitting outside on the other side of an enquiries hatch, but visible from the office. He has obviously been sitting there some time.*

CHRISTINE: He's looking for someone called Iris. Have we got an Iris? I can't think of an Iris. Stanley.

STANLEY: What?

CHRISTINE: Nice face.

STANLEY: Don't look at him, Christine. If you don't look at him he'll happen go away.
  (*Pause.*)

CHRISTINE: Stanley.

STANLEY: What?

CHRISTINE: He's still there.
  (*She smiles at* LEE.)

STANLEY: Course he's still there with you doing all that silly smiling. Christine.

CHRISTINE: What?

STANLEY: Wasn't that Iris in Despatch?

CHRISTINE: Which?

STANLEY: She was in Despatch. She had a big mauve jumper. Her mother had a duodenal ulcer. They had a caravan at Skipsea. Did she have a caravan at Skipsea?

LEE: Iris.

STANLEY: Her mother didn't have a duodenal ulcer? Ran a little primrose mini. Crippled with indigestion.

CHRISTINE: He may not have met her mother.

STANLEY: She could have told him.

CHRISTINE: She mightn't. If you're going out with somebody

241

you don't kick off by saying, "My mother's got a duodenal ulcer and we've got a caravan at Skipsea." That's quite far on in the relationship.

STANLEY: Anyway I think that was Eirlys not Iris.

CHRISTINE: Men, they don't want to know about your mother. You tell them your mother's got a duodenal ulcer and that puts the tin hat on it straightaway.

STANLEY: You'll find somebody one day, Christine. Raymond's not the only pebble on the beach.

CHRISTINE: I just wish I'd not splashed out on all that motorcycle gear.

STANLEY: Well, I thought you were being rather short-sighted at the time.

CHRISTINE: Mind you, they make motor bikes, don't they?

STANLEY: Who?

CHRISTINE: The Japanese. Honda. Suzuki.

STANLEY: He doesn't look particularly motorized to me. I just wish he'd go away. There'll be the Chairman of the CBI coming round in five minutes reconnoitring and we've got Aladdin stuck there. Have you no other data?

LEE: Iris.

CHRISTINE: Stanley. We could always ask Mr Turnbull.

STANLEY: Yes. I could always put my head in the gas oven.

CHRISTINE: Mr Turnbull knows everybody by name.

STANLEY: So do I. There's a Maureen in Maintenance. An Eileen in Records. Two Karens in Costing.

CHRISTINE: Debbie in the post room.

STANLEY: Diane in the canteen. Wait a minute. Canteen. Canteen, Christine. *Canteen*. We did use to have an Iris. She worked in the canteen before Mr Turnbull had the big clamp down. That's right. *Iris*. They caught her going through the gate with some cooking fat under her coat. Her locker was piled high with Carnation Milk. Iris.

LEE: Iris.

STANLEY: Don't get excited.

CHRISTINE: What happened to her?

STANLEY: She got finished. She was one of the first casualties of the Turnbull era. But her Dad works in the pressing shop. Butterworth. She's little Mr Butterworth's daughter. Iris Butterworth. Point him in the direction of the pressing shop. (*To* LEE) You want to be in the pressing shop. Off you go. Like the motto says: "The difficult we can do straightaway; the impossible takes time."

CHRISTINE: Come on, love.

(*She goes out and almost immediately* MR TURNBULL *comes in.*)

MR TURNBULL: Oh, yes, and who was that, the oriental gentleman?

STANLEY: A potential customer. Enquiring about delivery dates for South Korea.

MR TURNBULL: South Korea. There you are. Exactly what I was saying last week. It won't be long before the whole of the Middle East is knocking at the door.

(CHRISTINE *comes back and doesn't at first see* MR TURNBULL.)

CHRISTINE: I hope he finds her.

MR TURNBULL: Finds who?

26. INT. PRESSING SHOP. DAY

Some kind of machine shop. Not large. Noisy. Light engineering. About half-a-dozen MEN *working.* LEE *enters.*

ALF: We've got a visitor.

CYRIL: A trade delegation.

VIC: It's Mao Tse-tung. How do you do?

ALF: "New lamps for old."

(*All this above the noise of the machines.*)

Who is it you want? Who . . . do . . . you . . . want?

(LEE *shows him his paper.* ALF's *face changes. Stops his machine. Shows it to* VIC *who stops his. Gradually the machines shut down. There is silence.*)

Iris Butterworth?

LEE: Yes. Iris. Iris.

ALF: Iris Butterworth doesn't work here. Her Dad works here. Iris's Dad.

VIC: He works here all right. Where is he?

CYRIL: He's just paying a call.

VIC: Lucky for you.

ALF: I'd better tell him.

(ALF *goes to knock on the door of the toilet.*)

CYRIL: Alf. Wait on. You'd not better. You know Duggie.

VIC: Tell him, Alf. Go on.

CYRIL: No. Nay, Victor, have a heart.

VIC: Don't be soft.

CYRIL: Listen, you'd better go quick, you.

LEE: Iris. Iris's father.

CYRIL: Yes, Iris's father.

VIC: Go on, Alf.

(ALF *knocks on the door and* VIC *joins in the conversation.*)

ALF: Duggie. You've got a visitor.

DUGGIE: (*Through the door*) What?

ALF: You've got a visitor.

DUGGIE: Who? I'm on the lav.

VIC: (*Winking*) He wants your Iris.

DUGGIE: Who wants who?

VIC: Your Iris. This feller. There's a feller here wants your Iris. I want to see this.

DUGGIE: What sort of a feller?

VIC: A feller. You'd better stand back. He's a bloody tornado.

(*Sound of a lavatory flushing. The door of the toilet opens very slowly. A small timid* MAN *comes out, slowly fastening his braces.*)

DUGGIE: What about our Iris?

ALF: This feller wants her.

DUGGIE: Him?

VIC: Him.

DUGGIE: The Chink? Iris?

LEE: Iris.

VIC: (*Mimicking him*) Ilis.

CYRIL: Nay, Victor. He can't help the way he talks.

DUGGIE: You, is it? You. Do you know who I am?

LEE: No.

DUGGIE: I'm Iris's father. Are you the one, then? Are you him?
You're him, aren't you?

LEE: Him?

DUGGIE: The one she's been knocking about with.

VIC: He's one of these Disco Desmonds, Duggie.

DUGGIE: That's right, Victor. I thought his sort were generally
Maltese.

VIC: What Duggie?

DUGGIE: Pimps, Victor.

CYRIL: Nay, Duggie.

DUGGIE: Or else it's drugs. Is that it, drugs? Are you the last
link in the chain? Tibet to Scarborough. The outlet.

VIC: Bite his ankles, Dug.

DUGGIE: I expect you're getting her hooked, are you? The
opium, is it? I've seen them. The dull light in their eyes.
All purpose gone. Scum. Scum.

LEE: No. Iris.

VIC: I think he's making fun of you, Douglas, pulling your leg,
taking the Chinese piss.

DUGGIE: She never let on he was Chinese. Else I'd have given
her another hiding. You've got a nerve coming round here.
What do you want?

VIC: Her hand in marriage.

DUGGIE: Marriage doesn't mean anything to these people,
Victor. They just go behind a bush. Then they come
over here and expect us to do likewise. She was a
good girl.

CYRIL: She was a grand girl.

DUGGIE: Where is she now?

LEE: (*Nodding*) Where?

DUGGIE: You little slant-eyed tup. If I thought you were worth it I'd give you the hiding of your life.

VIC: I would. Me, I would, Duggie.

DUGGIE: Victor, I would not soil my fingers.

VIC: Put his head in the machine press, Duggie.

DUGGIE: It's not his head I want to put in the machine press, Victor.

CYRIL: Nay, Duggie. He looks as if he might be a nice lad, underneath.

DUGGIE: Underneath what?

CYRIL: Their different customs. He probably doesn't know any better.

DUGGIE: You wouldn't be saying that if he came sniffing round your Christine.

(LEE *takes the paper with Iris's name on it from* DUGGIE's *trembling fingers.*)

You see, look at him. He's shameless. No shame.

LEE: I am looking for Iris.

VIC: The nerve, Douglas. Of all the Chinese nerve. Clock him one.

LEE: Where is she?

DUGGIE: Don't ask me where she is. I know where her mother is. In her grave. With a broken heart. Iris. She's a scrubber. She's a bloody scrubber. (*Starts crying.*) My daughter's a bloody scrubber.

CYRIL: Nay, she's not.

DUGGIE: What do you know about it, you soft article.

ALF: (*To* LEE) You've upset him now. It's you that's done that. He was as right as rain till you came in. Coming in, upsetting him. You've no business. He's highly strung. He's on tablets.

CYRIL: I should take your teeth out, you'll feel better.

DUGGIE: I don't want to take my teeth out. I thought I'd seen everything when she fetched home a bloody Zambian. Now it's Wishee-Washee. Where did we go wrong, Betty? Where did we go wrong?

CYRIL: I think the nuns do the damage. It's all right when they're right little, but come puberty they allus break out. Look at Carmen Lockwood.

DUGGIE: Nuns? Nuns? She's never been near no nuns, Iris.

CYRIL: She went to Crossgates. Crossgates is nuns.

DUGGIE: It never is. Crossgates is comprehensive.

CYRIL: But nuns comprehensive.

DUGGIE: It isn't nuns. How many more times? There were no flaming nuns.

CYRIL: Sorry. My mistake.

DUGGIE: Nuns. Chinks. What a day.

VIC: And he's just standing there, the cause of the chaos.

DUGGIE: Doesn't he understand? I've disowned her. She is not my daughter. There is no person called Iris in my life.

CYRIL: It's tragic because she was a wonderful girl. Loved the open air.

ALF: I blame television.

DUGGIE: She never watched television. She was never in for long enough. She'd come in after her work, plaster herself up with make-up, then get off out to a disco or something similar, then pole in at half-past two in the morning. Well, I tell you, I don't care. It serves her right. Scrubbing floors in the hospital. Running errands for Paki doctors. That's all she's fit for. A hospital skivvy, Chiang Kai-shek, that's what Iris is. One of these ancillary workers.

LEE: Hospital?

DUGGIE: Yes, *hospital*. You want Iris, go up the Royal and look round the gerry wards. That's what she's doing, emptying slops, cleaning out bedpans. And it's all she's fit for. My daughter.

(*The boss has come in. It is the* MR TURNBULL *who came into Reception.*)

MR TURNBULL: Hello. I thought I was coming into the pressing shop. I find myself in a church. Silent. All activity at a standstill. One machine, idle. Another machine, idle. Idle, idle, idle. Are we getting the country back on its feet? Is this the year of the beaver? It seems not. It seems not. And you. What are you doing still on the premises? What do you want? To ruin our schedules? Bugger up our norms? You're not another one from ASLEF are you? Because I can't understand what you are doing here. Get out. Get out get out, get out, get out, get out. Do I make myself plain? I am saying to you, "Get out." And don't smile at me. Not funny. Not funny, not funny, not funny, not funny.

(*He ushers* LEE *through the factory and out.*)

A thought strikes me. You haven't been sent round to check on the fire precautions? No. Such subtlety is beyond the municipality. Carry on, Miss Dunbar. I'm just seeing this person off the premises. Do not come back. Come back do not. No. Not back here. Come, no. Out. Off.

LEE: Where is the hospital?

MR TURNBULL: What hospital? No hospital. All hospital. This place is a hospital. The sick, the lame, the halt. Bedridden. Work? Nowhere. Work, the disease. We cure them of it. That's what this place is, a hospital. Sick, sick, sick. We're all sick.

(MR TURNBULL *goes off muttering to himself.* LEE *goes, very sadly. England is mad.*)

27. INT. COFFEE SHOP. DAY

Cut to a smart culinary shop. Elizabeth David pots, teacloths, wooden utensils, etc. One part of it is a coffee place. LEE *sits there. Most of this scene is shot on him, his increasingly doleful face. Perhaps a tear even as the scene goes on.*

JANE, *who runs the shop, is talking to* LIZ.

JANE: The genesis of this place, the germ of the whole thing, I mean, the real seed, as it were, was when I was trying to find a decent double-boiler. You know, just an ordinary *bain-marie*. I scoured the whole of the town, and nobody's even *heard* of them. Which is ridiculous because they've been making double-boilers since the dawn of civilization, practically. So one night I said to Geoffrey, "Look, Geoffrey, I can't find a double-boiler for love nor money. You've got your pension and I've got those few pennies Aunty Lucy left me, adventure is the spice of life, why don't we blue it all on a shop that sells them. I mean, not exclusively. Other things as well. And that was how the whole thing started. Of course we've branched out a lot. Lots of pots, mostly French, you know, sort of thing you used to be able to pick up for a few francs any town in France any market day. Cost a bit more now, alas. But still heaps better than anything you get here. And, you know, I don't think I'm being fanciful, I think they make the food taste different. Then Geoffrey came up with the idea of making this little back place we had in the shop into a tea/coffee place served in the crocks we have on sale in the shop, open sandwiches, little snacks, cakes, etc., all strictly of the home-made variety . . . which we did . . . and, you know . . . it's become quite a little meeting place. It's called the Pop In because . . . well . . . you know that's what people do . . . just pop in . . . except old Geoff says it's called Pop In because Pop's always in, which he is, he has to be, look after the place . . . he's actually out just this minute, popped along to the bank, popped in there, ha ha, drawing out not depositing, because there's no money in it, we manage of course but what I think is that we perform a service. Then Vanessa helps out.

(*A very miserable* GIRL *is washing up*.)

I mean, I pay her a wage, but she does it very much on a friendly basis. Nice girl. Nervous. Bit anorexic. At least she doesn't eat the cakes. But, you know, the really satisfying thing is that one feels one is fulfilling a social need, and old Geoff says the same, because that's always been a big strong point with him. I mean, that's what the army was, really, you know, performing a service. I mean, I don't think there are enough little places like this, you know, *nice* places, places where the pots are nice and the cakes are nice and the people are nice. Where, really, you know, it's nice. So one does feel one is making a contribution and even taking into account VAT (which does make one's life sheer misery) even including VAT I think it's been worthwhile. (*To* LEE, *who is going*) Coffee and one cake. 75p.

LEE: Where is the hospital?

JANE: Are you ill?

LEE: Tell me the way to the hospital.

JANE: There are lots of hospitals. The Royal's at the top of the hill. Do you mean the Royal?

LEE: The hospital.

LIZ: He means the Royal.

JANE: Try the Royal.

    (LEE *goes out.*)

    Was he crying? I thought he was crying. I didn't think they did cry. I thought that was the point about them.

28. INT. HOSPITAL SLUICE ROOM. DAY

The sluice room off a hospital ward. A WOMAN ORDERLY *is washing up bedpans and bottles. Another* ORDERLY *comes in.*

FIRST ORDERLY: You work in a hospital and they think you're anybody's. I'm always finding that. Soon as I told him what I did he just went mad. No please or thank you.

SECOND ORDERLY: It's the body. They think you're not shocked by the body. They think you've seen it all.

FIRST ORDERLY: Well, I'm not shocked by the body, but I still like to be treated like a human being. It can get so clinical.

SECOND ORDERLY: I wish mine had been more clinical. He kept wanting a running commentary. Who was he?

FIRST ORDERLY: Smallish feller. Bit on the ginger side. Said he ran a string of dry cleaners.

SECOND ORDERLY: I've heard that before.

(FIRST ORDERLY *goes out and comes back straightaway*.)

FIRST ORDERLY: You seen Iris?

SECOND ORDERLY: Not on this afternoon. It's Tuesday.

FIRST ORDERLY: There's a little Chink wants her.

SECOND ORDERLY: A little Chink?

(*She goes and has a peep at* LEE, *dejectedly waiting*.)
No. That won't be for that Iris. He looks too nice for her.
It'll be the other Iris. Our Iris. They're students. They send
them round visiting. Lonely students they send round
seeing lonely old folks. Like Bob-a-Job. Not Bob-a-Job.
What do I mean? Samaritans. Something voluntary. I'll see
to him. Come on, love. Follow me.

LEE: Iris?

SECOND ORDERLY: Yes, Iris is here.

29. INT. HOSPITAL WOMEN'S WARD. DAY

MRS BEEVERS, *a woman in her sixties, is wearing a little bedjacket
and being visited by her husband.*

MRS BEEVERS: I've watched her picking her nose all afternoon.
It's just been pick pick pick. She's in with one of these
unwanted pregnancies. Have you brought me anything?

MR BEEVERS: Yes. I brought you the parish magazine.

MRS BEEVERS: Parish magazine! *Food*. Have you brought me
any food?

MR BEEVERS: Nay, Daisy, you're on a strict diet.

MRS BEEVERS: You love this, don't you? Watching me tortured.
I could murder a Kunzle cake.

(*The* SECOND ORDERLY *brings* LEE *down the ward to the bed
opposite* MRS BEEVERS *in which there is an* OLD LADY
asleep.)

SECOND ORDERLY: Iris. Iris. Wake up, love. Come on, sleeping
beauty, here's the prince.

LEE: No. No.

MRS BEEVERS: Go on, love. Wake her up. Iris. Iris. Don't let
her sleep. It's months since she had anybody to see her.

Iris! She's got two daughters and they never come near and
one of them's in a real tip-top job with Hotpoint. Come on,
Iris. Shake her.

OLD IRIS: What?

MRS BEEVERS: Got a visitor.

OLD IRIS: Where?

MRS BEEVERS: Here. Him. This young man.

OLD IRIS: Him? He's a Jap.

MRS BEEVERS: She forgets. Sit down a minute, love. She'll
come round in a bit. She'll surface eventually. Mind you,
she's not been all that clever. In fact she died last week.
They got the priest to come and give her the last rites and
do you know five minutes later they're along with the
trolley to resuscitate her. It's what I was saying to you (*her
husband*) hospitals, there's no liaison.

OLD IRIS: Are you one of these Japs? I didn't know I knew any
Japs. It just shows you who you come across. You're not
from our Gerald, are you? He was in a Jappy camp during
the war. He came out a skeleton.

MRS BEEVERS: That's all done with now. They've turned over a
new leaf. They make television sets. Our Bertram's got a
Jap car. (*To her* HUSBAND) Fancy coming to see Iris. This
is Iris. And I'm Daisy. All we want now is a Buttercup and
we'd be a right bunch.

OLD IRIS: Nay, Buttercup's a cow's name.

MRS BEEVERS: Ay, well. (*Peals of laughter.*) You've got some
nice hair. Hasn't he, Bert? Got nice hair? My sister-in-law's
hair was a bit like yours.

MR BEEVERS: Only she wasn't Japanese.

MRS BEEVERS: I wasn't saying she was. I'm just saying her hair
was on a par with his.

MR BEEVERS: He looks a bit lost to me.

MRS BEEVERS: Well, he'll be a student. He'll be one of these
foreign students.

OLD IRIS: He's not to do with the blackie vicar, is he?

MRS BEEVERS: No. We've got this black vicar comes round. He's Black and yet he's Church of England. But beautifully spoken. And lovely hands. Course it's all in the melting pot now, isn't it? Foreign doctors. Black vicars. The physio's Hungarian and Muriel over there, she has a home help that comes from Poland.

MR BEEVERS: Not every week? (MRS BEEVERS *looks at him.*) Comes from Poland. Not every week.

MRS BEEVERS: Is that a joke? It's all right, isn't it? I'm lying here with suspected gallstones and you're on top of the world. (*Pause.*) I bet the house is upside down.

MR BEEVERS: It never is. I did the kitchen floor this morning.

MRS BEEVERS: Which bucket did you use?

MR BEEVERS: The red one.

MRS BEEVERS: That's the outside bucket. I shall have it all to do again. Men, they make work.
(LEE *is sitting there unhappily. He looks at his chocolates, looks at* OLD IRIS, *who has dropped off again, and gives her the chocolates.*)
Isn't that nice? See, Iris. He's fetched you some chocolates. He's fetched some chocolates. (*Gets smartly out of bed.*) Are they Jappy chocolates?

MR BEEVERS: Nay, they're Dairy Box.

MRS BEEVERS: They're probably Jappy Dairy Box. That's what they do, pinch our labels and make their own. Let's have a look.

OLD IRIS: No. They're mine. He fetched them for me. Reparations.

MRS BEEVERS: Well, let me undo them for you. She'll be all day wrestling with the Cellophane.

OLD IRIS: I can't do with hard ones.

MRS BEEVERS: What's the index say?

OLD IRIS: Coffee creams are the ones I like. I'd have them all coffee creams.

MRS BEEVERS: That's coffee cream.

OLD IRIS: It never is. Bloody nugget.

(*She chucks it away and* MRS BEEVERS *gives her another*.)

MRS BEEVERS: You want to squat these, Iris. Get them in your locker quick. Do you want one, Bert? They won't last five minutes in here. Somebody's on the pinch. I think it's the nurses. I know one thing: every time I go to spend a penny the level of my Lucozade drops.

OLD IRIS: Hand round the hard ones. Save us the soft ones.

(MRS BEEVERS *makes to give one to* LEE.)

Don't give him one. I don't know him. Who is this Jappy feller?

MRS BEEVERS: He brought you the chocolates.

OLD IRIS: I thought they had a funny taste.

MRS BEEVERS: Hand them round, love, go on.

(LEE *hands round the chocolates, going round the beds*.)

Nice-looking young feller. Still, it'll take more than Dairy Box to erase the memory of Pearl Harbor.

(*The West Indian* STAFF NURSE *enters*.)

STAFF NURSE: Do you bin mind informin me what you is doin distributin de chocolates round de beds, man? En diabetics, man. En no sugar. Dis lady to whom you give de chocolates she bin in a coma last week cos some lady take pity on her and done give her some jelly, man. I jus don resuscitatin her man. I don wan to re-resuscitate her. We're in a short-staffin situation, man.

LEE: I want Iris.

STAFF NURSE: Don't rubbish me, man. Iris . (*Goes over to her*.)

Iris, gel. You en no friend of Iris, man. You in doin her no good turn. Wi de Dairy Box.

MRS BEEVERS: He gave us all some, didn't he, Bert? He fair insisted. I told him I was on a strict diet, but he wouldn't take no for an answer.

MR BEEVERS: They can't, you see. It's to do with losing face.

STAFF NURSE: (*While trying to fetch* OLD IRIS *round*.)

Resuscitatin and re-resuscitatin, I don wan de doctors

crawlin round my neck all de time. Am I on de bum or de bonce. What you doin on de ward anyway? En no visitin hours. En no relation of Iris. Iris en no foreign relations. Out of here, Chinese man or I gwan call de biggest black man you ever seen in yo life, and he beat de shit out of you, man, Third World or no Third World.
(LEE *leaves hurriedly.*)

30. EXT. HOTEL STAFF ENTRANCE. DAY
LEE *going dejectedly in at the staff entrance.*

31. INT. HOTEL CORRIDOR. DAY
Along the narrow up-and-down corridor towards his room. He stops at his own door, then goes to one opposite and knocks. He knocks again.
BERNARD: (*Out of vision*) Yes.
LEE: It's me. Lee.
BERNARD: (*Out of vision*) Hold on.

32. INT. BERNARD'S BEDROOM. DAY
After a bit BERNARD *opens the door. He has a towel round his waist. He nips smartly back into bed once* LEE *comes in. There is a blowsy* GIRL *in bed, and there are a pair of bright yellow boots in the corner.*
LEE: Hello.
GIRL: Hello.
LEE: I did not find her. Iris. I could not find her.
BERNARD: I know you didn't find her. Course you didn't find her. This is her. This is him. Iris, Lee. Lee, Iris.
IRIS: Pleased to meet you. (*Whispering*) Who?
BERNARD: The one I was telling you about. You know. Olive skin.
IRIS: Oh. Him.
BERNARD: She came round here after work. Came round for tea, didn't you? Tea, bread and butter, scones and jam. Plus something from the trolley.

255

LEE: I went to many places. Nobody knows her.

BERNARD: Nobody knows Iris? Everybody knows Iris. Don't they, Iris?

IRIS: Oh, yes. They all know me.

BERNARD: You can't have gone to the right place. He can't have gone to the right place.

(*She turns over on her stomach and mutters.*)

What?

IRIS: I wouldn't have fancied him anyway.

BERNARD: No? He's a nice lad, aren't you, Genghis? Shy, but nice.

IRIS: I think they're a bit creepy.

(*She turns over and looks at him boldly.* BERNARD *also.* LEE *goes.*)

33. INT. LEE'S BEDROOM. DAY

LEE *lies on his bed, having taken everything off except his underpants. His hand moves slowly down his body to rest on his thigh.*

34. INT. HOTEL DINING ROOM. EVENING

Both WAITERS *on duty.* LEE *with the sweet trolley. The dining room is very busy and full of diners. Credits over.*